The Fourth Degree of Prayer

The Fourth Degree of Prayer

MICHAEL C. VOIGTS

CASCADE *Books* · Eugene, Oregon

THE FOURTH DEGREE OF PRAYER

Cascade Books
An Imprint of Wipf and Stock Publishers
199 W. 8th Ave., Suite 3
Eugene, OR 97401

www.wipfandstock.com

PAPERBACK ISBN: 978-1-5326-8879-9
HARDCOVER ISBN: 978-1-5326-8880-5
EBOOK ISBN: 978-1-5326-8881-2

Cataloging-in-Publication data:

Names: Voigts, Michael C., author.
Title: The fourth degree of prayer / Michael C. Voigts
Description: Eugene, OR : Cascade Books, 2022 | Includes bibliographical references.
Identifiers: ISBN 978-1-5326-8879-9 (paperback) | 978-1-5326-8880-5 (hardback) | 978-1-5326-8881-2 (ebook)
Subjects: 1. Prayer—Christianity. 2. Spiritual life—Christianity.
Classification: BV210.2 .V59 2022 (print) | BV210.2 (ebook)

for Jerry

Table of Contents

Introduction

THE DARK SKY SLOWLY lightened and a new day was being born. The dark valley was coming to life once again. Although the sun would eventually take over and turn the air into an unbreathable thickness, the early morning was already humid. As he did every day, Jake wondered if this would be the last sunrise over the steep mountains he'd ever see. Perhaps he wouldn't have to endure the torture from the elements or from his Japanese prison guards much longer. Their daily humorous threats of potentially putting a bullet in his head made each laborious day in China seem like his last.

As with the seven other American prisoners of war in this camp, Jake's B-25 had run out of fuel in April 1942, somewhere over the Chinese wilderness. He had been part of an American response to the Japanese attack on Pearl Harbor a few months before. They completed their mission over Nagoya, Japan and ditched their planes before being found by Japanese military personnel. The Americans were tortured, starved, and psychologically abused. Three were shot and another died of starvation.

Jake DeShazer didn't share the devout faith of his parents. While growing up in Oregon he went to worship every Sunday, but only to keep peace in the house. His interests were in other, more mechanical pursuits. Jake's mother was a woman of prayer. He admired her faithfulness in spending so much time in prayer, but he didn't understand where those prayers went, other than simply vanishing into the air. Yet, he couldn't escape the memory that on that fateful night when he parachuted from the B-25, he had a sense that he wasn't alone. At the time he imagined it was merely his mind attempting to comfort him. Years later he would discover that at that very moment he had been falling from the sky, his mother had been on her knees praying for her unconverted son, interceding for him. An American in the solitary confinement hut next to Jake's was a Christian.

Jake remembers his fellow prisoner whispering to him one night, "When we make it out of here, we're going to realize that Jesus was the reason for all of this." That friend died a few days later.

When the guards were ordered by their superiors to distribute a single Bible to the prisoners to keep them psychologically at ease, Jake's interest in reading was simply having something to read to pass the time until his next beating. He read a few passages that didn't really mean much to him until he flipped a few pages ahead and discovered Luke 23:34. As Jesus was enduring abuse from the Roman guards while hanging on the cross, he said, "Father, forgive them, for they know not what they do." At that moment, Jake felt an overwhelming sense of peace that he knew could only have come from the God of his parents. The only reason these Japanese guards were treating him so cruelly was that they didn't know who Jesus was. In that moment, Jake surrendered his life to the Jesus in that Bible and began to see the world—and his situation—with a different set of eyes. He began feasting on the words of the Bible, not knowing when it would be taken from him to be given to another prisoner.

As Jake was beaten, starved, and tortured over the next three years, he was able to endure by repeating Luke 23:34 over and over in his mind. The anger that he had previously felt toward the Japanese was replaced with sympathy for their spiritual ignorance. He began treating the Japanese with kindness, which he found was reciprocated. And on August 20, 1945, the sky above the camp was filled with American paratroopers who had come to liberate the surviving Army Air Corps personnel. Jake had endured the war as a prisoner in the jungle for forty months.

Upon being discharged from the Army, Jake and the others were lauded and proclaimed national heroes. They were on the cover of *Life* magazine and made grand marshals of what seemed like countless parades. He had several job offers, but he couldn't escape what he knew was God's calling on his life. After finishing college and then seminary, Jake spent the next several decades as a Christian missionary in Japan, preaching to and living with the people who had once tortured him. During that time, he met and baptized Mitsuo Fuchida, the Japanese pilot who had led the raid on Pearl Harbor. He also planted a church in Nagoya, the city he had bombed back in 1942.

In 2003, I found myself in Salem, Oregon, standing before a small housing unit in an unremarkable retirement community. In my capacity as the alumni director at Asbury Theological Seminary, I was there on behalf of the school where Jake prepared for mission work, to offer our thanks for his many years of faithful Christian service. Personally, however, I wanted to sit at the feet of a Christian hero to learn what motivated him for decades of life with those who had treated him so horribly. When the ninety-one-year-old man finally made his way to the door to introduce himself to me, I found standing before me not a giant of the Christian faith, but a humble, peaceful man whose hospitality began before he even said "hello." Florence, his beloved wife and ministry partner, had died a few years earlier, so he was alone in this unassuming apartment. On his walls were not his medals and awards ("They're in the closet if you'd like to see them," he said) but pictures of his family and Japanese friends. He spoke quietly, methodically, and with an authentic, sweet love for God and others. We met for about an hour, and although he never revealed it, I could discern it was time for his tired body to take his afternoon nap. Before I left, we prayed for each other. Jake's prayer for me had a supernatural depth I still cannot explain. In fact, it didn't seem to come from him at all, but from the angels in the throne room of heaven. As he walked me to the door, I sensed he was still in prayer. In fact, I realized that he was in prayer the entire time I was with him. Although he was speaking with me, his conversation was with God.

As I drove north to Portland later that afternoon to catch my flight back to Kentucky, my soul was grieving. For ten years I had been a pastor in local churches and was now a "pastor" to the graduates of my seminary, yet I was in pain. My relationship with God did not have the magnitude of Jake's. I had ministry aspirations, writing projects, and further academic goals. My idea of a successful ministry was akin to the final words a dying family member said to me when I was a teenager: "Now go show the world what you can do." What was it about Jake's relationship with God that gave him the courage and peace to survive that prison camp and then share the gospel with the people who had imprisoned him? How could a national hero live such an unassuming life of peace and obscurity? How could Jake have been in prayer even as he was having a conversation with me?

This is a book about prayer, but it's also a book about holy living. In fact, I'm not sure one can exist without the other. Does holy living encourage prayer, or does prayer encourage holy living? Perhaps, as John Calvin writes regarding knowledge of self and knowledge of God, the order is not as important as the realization of both in one's life.[1] When we pray, we're inviting God into the depths of our lives, where no other person has been. If

1. Calvin, *Institutes*, I.1.

this life with God is authentic, it's naturally going to result in a different way of seeing and experiencing the world. Similarly, when we see the world with the eyes of God, then wanting to spend quality time with God becomes natural rather than something we need to schedule so we don't forget.

Seeing the world as it really is may be difficult for those Christians who are so absorbed with what the world offers that they cannot even realize how soaking wet they are. William Blake, in his classic work *The Marriage of Heaven and Hell*, writes that if the doors of our perception were cleansed, then we'd be able to see the world as it really is, which he calls "Infinite." If we are to understand ourselves as God created us, a healthy understanding of God and of God's world must be part of the equation.

As we will explore in this little book, prayer is much more than words we say or thoughts we think to God. Prayer is more than incorporating the key elements of any proper prayer (adoration, confession, thanksgiving, supplication). Prayer is also more than waiting with expectation for God to speak to us. Prayer, when properly understood, encompasses all of ourselves: our nature, our activities, our loves, our emotions, and our motivations. In the words of Rose Marie Dougherty, prayer "has more to do with our wanting God and God's wanting us than any skill we might acquire."[2] In these pages I propose four degrees, or levels, of prayer that are available to all people. I believe all people, regardless of belief or unbelief in this or that worldview, are created in the image of God (Genesis 1:26–27). Spiritual anthropology is as foundational as sound theology in any discussion of Christian prayer. Because God created humanity to have a relationship with God, we are incomplete until we (to paraphrase Augustine) find our rest in God. Like many of the church fathers, Gregory of Nyssa describes human nature as the image of God in our capacity to have both rational and spiritual dynamics, including free will.[3] Conversely, the church fathers are generally unanimous that the likeness of God in humans refers to the virtues of God's holy love, which we might obtain only through Jesus Christ and by the Holy Spirit. Irenaeus, for example, wrote that in the fall, humanity lost the likeness of God yet retained the image of God.[4] These anthropological foundations are imperative in a discussion of prayer and a prayerful life, for knowing who we are as collective human beings helps us know to what capacity interaction with Almighty God is available to us.

---

2. Dougherty, *Group Spiritual Direction*, 29.

3. Gregory, "On the Creation of Man," III.2.

4. Irenaeus, *Against Heresies*, 466.

I have one warning before we take the plunge: Once we discover what the role of prayer can be in our lives, there is no going back to a previous way of seeing ourselves, the world, and God. Once we discover the reality of prayer's depths we never knew existed, the Holy Spirit will show us just how elementary our previous understanding of prayer really was. Some of what you'll read in this book may disrupt your walk with God. As I've done on occasion, you may read something that makes you want to throw this book across the room. You may read this book and discover for the first time the depths to which God wants to be in relationship with you. Let the prayer of Ambrose be ours as we begin: "Let, then, this water, O Lord Jesus, come into my soul and into my flesh, that through the moisture of this rain the valleys of our minds and the fields of our hearts may grow green."[5]

5. Ambrose, *On the Holy Spirit*, I.16.

Acknowledgments

BECAUSE THE NATURE OF prayer itself is communal, involving a person and God, a healthy perspective of prayer should model the participatory influence of others. Therefore, attempting to write a book on prayer from one's own experience alone would be foolishness. Without the wisdom bestowed upon me by saints on earth as well as those who are alive and well in heaven, the composition of this little book would have been impossible.

I'd like to thank my sisters and brothers in Christ of the Lay Cistercians of Gethsemani Abbey. Through our monthly meetings, their spiritual insights and love for others have become a conduit for the Holy Spirit in my life. I'm also thankful for the monks of Gethsemani for making this Protestant feel at home in their midst. They personify the best of what encapsulates the ecumenical body of Christ.

I'd also like to express appreciation to my faculty colleagues and students at Asbury Theological Seminary. They share my desire for *Divinarum humanumque rerum cognitio*, or the "knowledge of things Divine and human." My love for God continues to deepen through the presence of each one of them in my life. My editor, Brooke Harris, has turned these scratchings into something of worth, and I'm encouraged and thankful for her efforts.

The sacrifices my wife Sheryl has made on my behalf over the years are too numerous to include here. God continues to use her as a means of grace in my life.

Finally, I must express eternal thanks to the man who set me on this formational journey of the exploration of God, Asbury Theological Seminary Professor Emeritus Jerry L. Mercer. Jerry's life will always be the embodiment of the content of this book through his joyful love of Jesus. For thirty years he has been to me a professor, a spiritual mentor, and a friend.

1

Do We Love God?

ACCORDING TO A 2019 Pew Research report, 65 percent of Americans consider themselves Christians. This is down twelve percent over similar studies a decade earlier.[1] Similarly, a 2021 Gallup study revealed that for the first time in the organization's history, membership of churches, synagogues, and mosques dropped in the United States below 50 percent of the population.[2] Of course, religious identity is not the same as religious commitment. Greater still is the discrepancy between religious commitment and personal love for one's deity. The concept of loving God seems simple enough, especially in light of proponents of prosperity gospels, who preach that God rewards faithful people with financial benefits, contentment, peace, and the like. However, when understood in its fullest sense, the idea of loving God becomes more complex than merely expressing positive affection towards God. A relationship with God based on fear, obedience, and/or responsibility can only get us so far in a substantive, intimate relationship with the Lord. Without a deep love for God, we may find it difficult to engage in formative, prayerful conversations with God. Therefore, before we can move forward in discussing the potential depths of prayer in our lives, we have to begin with a general examination of the depths to which we love God right now.

1. Pew Research Center, "In U.S., Decline of Christianity."
2. Gallup, Inc., "U.S. Church Membership Falls."

What is "Love"?

The word *love* has become somewhat meaningless today. We love movies, pizza, God, sports teams, families, a nation, and other meaningful aspects of our lives, yet these uses for "love" have become so highly nuanced that the word itself becomes meaningless to us. Movies make us emotional. Pizza fills our taste buds with pleasure. God brings us completeness. Sports teams help us feel connected with others. Families and nations give us a sense of identity. The one similarity in all these life aspects is that they are self-referenced. They begin with ourselves and return to ourselves. When our love for God and our love for pizza both bring pleasure to our lives (albeit in different aspects), we must ask the question: Do we really know how to love God?

In the Old Testament, the word *ahavah*, commonly translated as "love," does not connote a feeling one has towards someone else. Instead, the direction is away from ourselves and into the life of someone else. It implies the idea of breathing for someone else. *Ahavah* is not a noun, but a verb. It is about giving of our time and efforts for someone else, forsaking how that might affect us. In Deuteronomy 6:5, we're instructed to "love the Lord your God with all your heart and with all your souls and with all your strength." Jesus refers to this passage in Matthew 22:37. It's clear that this use of the word *love* is not emotive, but active. This activity may begin with simple obedience, but by God's grace, it transitions into an all-encompassing motivation of our lives.

A true, biblical understanding regarding love for God is certainly not a self-referenced phenomenon (as our love for pizza might be). Love for God is beyond ourselves, manifest in our capacity to be a light in a dark world (Matthew 5:14), and offers spiritual fruit to nourish others (Galatians 5:22-23). Given this definition, when I look at various societies in the world (both secular and Christian), it seems pretty clear to me that not only do many of us not love God, we do not know how to love God. As we examine a life of prayer, our capacity to pray is directly related to the depth of our love for God.

One Way of Measuring Our Love for God

Because prayer is acutely connected with one's love for God, it may serve us to examine one person's approach to understanding human capacity to love God. In the twelfth century, Frenchman Bernard of Clairvaux wrote a small treatise entitled *On Loving God*. Some have called this little work the definitive extra-biblical text on human love for the Trinitarian God. Bernard writes that there are four progressive stages, or degrees, in how we love God. Every person, regardless of her or his knowledge of God or relationship with God, falls into one of these stages. As the Holy Spirit develops our love for God, we move from one stage to another.

In the first degree of love for God, Bernard writes that we love ourselves for the sake of ourselves. In this stage, individuals are focused solely on themselves in order to better themselves in the world. This may involve vocational/professional pursuits, sensual pleasures, material goods, or even simple egoism. People in this stage may appear to care for others, but it is only for their own selfish desires. Modern church growth scholars have coined these people as "unchurched" or "pre-Christian," although persons at this level may have been raised in the church but left it for the pursuit of their own accomplishments and desires. These people place themselves at the center of their world in order to accomplish that which will have the most benefit to themselves and their own life mission. In order to do this, people in this stage focus on self-improvement in any form: education, physical fitness, monetary security, family stability, entertainment, or other supposed ways to improve our standing, reputation, or happiness in the world.

While a focus on God does not play a role in this first degree, Bernard includes this as a degree of love for God due to his understanding of the nature of humanity: the *imago Dei*. When we love ourselves for the sake of ourselves, we make ourselves the god of our lives, for we become the center of our existence. We want other people to agree with us because we know better than they do. We strive to attain all this world has to offer, so we go into debt in order to have the latest material goods we believe will improve our lives. Deep down we know these products and electronic devices will not cure the emptiness of our hearts, but since our highest ideal is ourselves, we believe the lie.

When Steve Jobs introduced the first Apple iPad in 2010, he spent ninety minutes lauding how the iPad would change the lives of everyone who used it. He believed the iPad would positively affect the lives of everyone who owned one. He described it as "more intimate than a laptop, and so much more capable than a smartphone."[3] What Jobs didn't share

3. Jobs, "Apple Keynote Address."

to the adoring crowd is that he wouldn't allow his own children use one.[4] Although Jobs and others in the tech world understand the myth of technology, they disingenuously praise the products they make, knowing that technology can never help us move beyond ourselves and our desire for self-actualization.

When advertising campaigns encourage us to extend our personalities into the products we own, we move ourselves away from our humanity. Because we falsely identify ourselves by merchandise brands, sports teams, or social status, we actually move away from God in our disregard for our actual identity as the *imago Dei*. Dare I mention, the same false identity occurs when we identify ourselves by a sports team, political party, or Christian denomination. Local churches who define themselves by their style, ideology, technology, or even their activities have a misunderstanding of sound ecclesiology, resulting in a false understanding of themselves as the body of Christ. Whether it regards an individual or a congregation, we love ourselves for the sake of ourselves because we don't really understand ourselves. This makes a life of prayer virtually impossible.

Bernard of Clairvaux describes the second degree of love for God as loving God, but for our own sake. In this stage, we realize that God exists and we desire to have a relationship with God, but it is only to serve our own desires, including a fear of hell, self-fulfillment, or social appearances. Many of the people in this stage are actively involved in a local church and have a contagious Christian witness. What keeps us from moving out of this level of love for God is our concern for the sense of self-completion that a relationship with God brings to our lives.

Authors who encourage readers to find their purpose or mission in life can lead them no further than this degree of love for God, since finding one's purpose is a self-fulfilling quest. The temptation of denominations is for new Christians to be formed in their own image and traditions rather than forming new disciples in the image of Christ. Unfortunately, many Christians in North America are under the false impression that loving God for our own sake is the pinnacle of the Christian life and love for God. Instead, according to Bernard of Clairvaux, it's only half of the degree to which we're able to love God. Loving God in order to get something in return from God is love, but it is a selfish love. This is nothing more than a phrase attributed to Augustine and quoted by Martin Luther: *incurvatus in se*, or a turning inward upon oneself. Luther identifies this inward focus as

---

4. Alter, *Irresistible*, 1.

the result of original sin.[5] A life transformed by Christ has a love for God that turns that person out of oneself, or *incurvatus ex se*. Until we allow the Holy Spirit into the deepest recesses of our lives, our love for God will be limited to egocentric love.

Since God is love (1 John 4:8), God's being and activity are united in holy love towards us. Loving God unconditionally is the opposite of this second degree of love for God, in which we place expectations on our love for God. As a Cistercian monk once shared with me, "The moment we expect something from love, we've prostituted it." When our motivation to pray, serve others, or share the gospel is to bring fulfillment to our lives as disciples of Jesus, we've read (but haven't heard) Jesus' words in Matthew 16:24 to deny ourselves, take up our cross, and follow him.

Without any doubt, God can use selfish service for God's glory. However, it stunts our spiritual growth and limits our capacity to love God completely. It's difficult to escape the consumerism of this second degree of love for God because we're conditioned by cultures inside and outside of the body of Christ to see the world with a mirror instead of a lens. The reality is that our love for God is conditioned by our worldview. When we understand ourselves primarily as citizens of the kingdom of God, we're able to see beyond ourselves and our opinions, as our gaze is moved from ourselves to the glorious face of God. What differentiates this second degree of love for God from the third is the answer to this question from Luke 8:25: *Ubi est fides vestra?* "Where is your faith?" Phrased another way, "Where do you place your faith?" If we place our faith in our *experiences* with God, we become idolaters. However, placing our faith in God himself leads to the next degree of love for God.

In the third degree of love for God, Bernard asserts that we love God simply for the sake of God. In this stage of love for God, we love God without any thought of personal or spiritual benefit. We simply love God because of who God is. Bernard writes that "this love is pleasing because it is free." This love for God is free because it is not chained to any human desire. Persons who love God at this stage are freed from any aspect of self-fulfilling Christian discipleship. Bernard is not saying that this type of love for God is without benefits to the individual—surely life is more worth living when we live this way—but what he stresses is that when we love God this deeply, we do so without any personal objectives or ambitions. Some understand this type of love for God as resulting from a sanctified or holy

5. Luther, *Lectures on Romans*, 291.

life, attainable for every Christian who earnestly desires to place Christ first in his or her life.

When we love God in the third degree, we discover that seeking personal growth—even if it's spiritual growth—ultimately leads back to ourselves. Freed from this selfish endeavor, our relationship with Christ is like that of a loving spouse whose only desire is to please the other; they care nothing about getting something in return for their love. Simply being with their spouse is enough. A classic biblical example of this type of love is Psalm 131, in which the psalmist describes his soul like a weaned child in the arms of his mother. A weaned child is a child who is able to eat on her own, no longer needing nourishment from her mother. The psalmist expresses his love for God as one in which he needs nothing from God. Simply being with God is enough.

A man who had been a spiritual director in my life for many years had suffered with physical pain for decades. In his later years, the surgically implanted pain pump in his spine was not adequate to alleviate the agony in his back. For years, he never ceased praying that God would ease the pain in his back, but the pain only increased as he got older. In the many times I sat with him and inquired about his level of pain, his only response would be, "God is so beautiful. Isn't he wonderful?" Had I been in his situation, I probably would have responded a bit differently (and colorfully!). For this holy man, however, his love for God was not based on the condition of his life, but on the nature of who God is. God had not healed him of physical pain, yet in his mind God was still faithful and worthy of wonder.

Loving God in the third degree is about our perspective, not our situation. You might imagine how this stage of loving God affects our prayers. Rather than merely asking God for a list of wants and needs, the focus becomes the nature of who God is. Evelyn Underhill refers to this type of perspective as living with mystical eyes.[6] Try not to let that word *mystical* frighten you. Christian mysticism is nothing more than acknowledging the mystery of God and the world around us. For Underhill, it's seeing the world as it actually is, and not as secular humanists perceive it. This comes when we love God not to receive God's blessings, but simply because God is worthy of our love. My spiritual director, facing the real possibility of an imminent death, expressed his love for God this way: "I prayed this morning, 'Lord, when I stand before you, I don't care if you throw my sorry soul into the bowels of hell. All I humbly ask is that before you do, you

6. Underhill, *Practical Mysticism*, 29.

allow me to kiss your feet.'" This is not a man who doubted the assurance of his faith. Nothing could be further from the truth! Instead, his love for God was based not on his sure admission into heaven, but on the beauty of God's glorious nature. His unquestioned trust in God continued to bloom, even in moments of excruciating pain. Like the saints of old, he knew that physical pain is not the worst pain we can endure. The gravest type of pain is a loss of hope in God. Perhaps this is why the Christian who lives a life of prayer is surrounded by others. Christian community allows us to see how other people deal with pain, which helps put our own into perspective.

Trust is essential in any loving relationship, for we cannot love someone intimately unless we first trust them. A lack of trust results from fear and fear is one of the greatest obstacles to growth in Christ. Trusting in the goodness of God regardless of our life circumstances takes time to mature in our lives. Allowing the Holy Spirit to produce this trust in us requires us to be honest with ourselves. If we do not trust God in a given situation, it is better to be bluntly honest with God than attempt to deceive God, with platonic spiritual words. We've all placed trust in others only to face disappointment when that trust is broken. Transferring broken trust to God is often a reality in our lives we do not want to admit. However, when we come to God authentically in who we are and in who God is, our love for God has potential to result in an authentic, trust-bearing love; loving God for who God is and not for how God makes us feel.

How might the body of Christ today look if it exhibited this third degree of love for God? Large, aesthetically pleasing sanctuaries and megachurch facilities would become useless if Christians looked beyond the satisfaction of belonging to such impressive congregations. Christian product merchandising, denominationalism, and bureaucratic structures would need to be dismantled. Local church monetary distribution practices would shift. Billboards and expensive websites that advertise local churches would become obsolete. Seminary education would not become the equivalent of ministry trade schools, but institutions of higher education that focus on the theological and spiritual implications of the sacrifice of ministry and discipleship. This third degree of love for God is not a spiritual ideal for a few. It remains an expectation for all who call themselves disciples of Jesus.

While the third degree may seem like the pinnacle of human love for God, Bernard offers one more: We love ourselves for the sake of God. Upon first thought, this seems to be backtracking one or two degrees. However, understood properly, this level of human love for God is so lofty that only a few people on earth may be able to experience the grace attain it. Bernard himself described this degree of love as most likely occurring in heaven. According to Bernard, in this stage, individuals cannot even imagine themselves apart from God. When we comprehend ourselves as existing only in God, we are able to become fully realized of God's love for us. Some have likened this degree of love for God as a realization of Hebrews 6:1, in which the author exhorts, "let us go on to perfection." Many Christians, including Roman Catholics and those from the Wesleyan tradition, believe that Christian perfection is attainable in this life. John Wesley used the term "entire sanctification" to describe this phenomenon, whereas Catholic writers have used the term "spiritual union with God."[7] Regardless of the nomenclature, the aggregation of meanings imply a state of being that resembles Christ rather than the culture around us, made possible by the indwelling of the Holy Spirit. John of the Cross wrote that when we enter these deepest aspects of love for God, it is because the Holy Spirit has purified, quieted, and strengthened our lives in such a way that we are able to experience this spiritual unity with God.[8]

The concepts involved in this fourth degree of love for God are mystical and complex. Bernard describes this love for God as occurring when "human feelings melt in a mysterious way and flow into the will of God."[9] Considering the busy lives most of us lead, Bernard's description may seem unattainable, as God cannot be all in all to us unless we give everything of ourselves to God. How might we honestly give 100 percent of ourselves to God when so many responsibilities fill our lives? As we'll see in the pages that follow regarding prayer in the fourth degree, this level of love for God may not be as unattainable as it first appears. However, we must learn to be patient with ourselves and with God as we grow to process the great profound truth of life with God: We have the divine in us.

The Relationship Between Love for God and Prayer

As the title of this chapter indicates, the simple sentence "I love God" is not so simple. When we state that we love God, our declaration implicitly involves our motivations, any unhealed emotional wounds from our past, current theological misconceptions of the nature of God, and our understanding

7. By "union with God," I do not intend *theosis*, which is addressed in chapter 5.
8. John of the Cross, *The Dark Night*, II:24.
9. Bernard, *On Loving God*, X.28.

of what it means to live in an authentic, trustworthy community. Scripture is clear that God loves us and desires to be in relationship with us. Like any relationship, this involves uninterrupted communication and a quantity of time. This is precisely why love for God and prayer are so intimately intertwined. When we are in love with someone, communication with them is effortless. We do not even need words to convey information. For example, when I have my eye on a delicious pastry I shouldn't have, my wife, Sheryl—with one look of her eye—can express multiple messages to me that tell me to back away because she loves me and knows that consuming that pastry is not the best decision for me. Decades of life that Sheryl and I have spent together allow us to speak to each other on multiple levels without having to rehearse the best way to say something.

Perhaps if we loved God this way, prayer would not be as intimidating to us as we make it out to be. Thoughts like, "What if I say the wrong thing?"; "What if my prayer isn't theologically sound?"; or "What if I sound stupid?" are indications of a relationship with God based not on deep, intimate love but on something else. When God is more to us than a mere deity we obey but our very life itself, prayer is not intimidating. Of course, we must acknowledge that as a Being greater than which nothing greater can be conceived, the transcendent, Almighty God, reigns over our lives. However, God is also immanent. He is Emmanuel, God with us. For Christians, God is even closer than that, for God's Spirit lives not just with us, but in us. Loving God involves an acknowledgment of who God is, a healthy understanding of who we are, and the implications of the two.

As we move into the chapters that follow, we will discover how these four degrees of love for God proposed by Bernard of Clairvaux actually parallel various degrees, or levels, of prayer. The role of prayer in our lives can be more than recitation of written words, or spontaneous mental meditations, or verbal construction of words. I would argue that most of us travel around the sun our entire lives without the realization that prayer can have a broad, formational role in our relationship with the Trinitarian God.

2

The Joy of Self-Discovery
(Prayer in the First Degree)

I FIRST SAW THE movie *Jaws* when I was ten years old. Like millions of others who were frightened by the prospect of being eaten alive by an unknown monster from the sea, I stayed out of the water. Unlike my family and friends, I stayed in the boat while they went water skiing and I played on the beach instead of in the waves. My fear was so real that in my mind it was absolutely conceivable for a shark to squeeze through the drain at the bottom of our swimming pool and attack me. I still swam in the pool, but I tried to stay away from the deep end and always kept an eye on that perilous drain.

Thankfully, my fears have waned. I now enjoy swimming when I'm afforded the opportunity and dream of wasting away days on the open water. When my wife and I went on a cruise several years ago, I loved to sit on the open-air deck and just watch and listen to the sea. The massive ship cutting through the clear blue water was cathartic for me. The cruise liner was constantly on the move, not sitting idle, taking us from one exotic location to another.

It was during one of the days in port that my eyes were opened to a world I almost missed, and it came from an event I never dreamed I would allow myself to experience: we went on a snorkeling excursion. I was about to enter the Caribbean Sea. There was no drain at the bottom of this body of water. No shallow end in this reef. Yet I knew I needed to overcome my fear; so without thinking and before I was even ready, I jumped into the crystal-clear water.

I was immediately overcome with a world I had only seen on You-Tube. I was a visitor without a passport in a foreign world of multicolored coral, dozens of species of tropical fish, flowery sea anemones, and even a solitary sea turtle. The sea I had grown to love from above wasn't the sea at all. What I had understood the sea to be wasn't a hundredth of what it really was. As we headed back to the cruise ship, I began to reflect on my snorkeling experience and my previous illogical fear of the water. Perhaps I wasn't ever fearful of hungry ocean creatures at all. What if my anxiety stemmed from a fear of looking below the surface of my own life to discover who I really was?

The first degree of prayer is the joy of self-understanding. Until we know who we are as God created us, it is going to be difficult for us to offer ourselves to God in love. This chapter is about putting on our spiritual snorkeling gear and taking a look at our lives. It's about looking at ourselves in a way that is far deeper than a surface-level understanding. God has created us as multidimensional persons. We are more than who we think we are. We are more than whom we love. We are more than what we do. Unfortunately, due to the influence of the secular (and sometimes Christian) culture around us, many of us find ourselves unable to comprehend who we even are.

The Living Well of Our Souls

Each of us has a well inside of us. That well is our soul. Our soul is that part of us that God created to make us who we are. It matters not what we do for a living, or the style of clothes we wear, or how physically in shape or attractive we are. Our soul defines us. Our soul is deep, and unless we can discover the richness of its depths, we never quite discover ourselves. In order to completely love God, we must understand ourselves—our real selves—and not who we are as the world defines us. In his classic work *The Imitation of Christ*, Thomas à Kempis writes, "A humble knowledge of yourself is a surer way to God than a profound searching after knowledge."[1] The more we seek knowledge, the more tempted we are to abuse that knowledge by allowing it to define us. This leads us down the destructive path to pride. Humility has been defined as having an honest opinion of ourselves because we know ourselves well. When we understand our temptations, our gifts, our tendencies, and other aspects of our lives, we

1. à Kempis, *Imitation of Christ*, I.3.4.

are able to approach God honestly without trying to hide anything from God. This helps us during times of frustration or difficulty, for we are able to know ourselves well enough to maneuver through such times by God's grace.

In Genesis 26, Abraham's son Isaac discovered that the Philistines had filled his wells with dirt. This was a problem, as the people were already experiencing a drought in the region. What made the situation even more shocking for Isaac is that the destroyed wells were actually dug by his father Abraham, so the destruction of them devastated part of Isaac's family identity and legacy. Isaac's response was to re-dig those wells, and he gave them the same names his father had given them. Throughout our lives, the world can fill the wells of our souls with dirt. Many times this process is so gradual, we don't even realize that it is happening. The well inside each of us is our identity, yet many of us never plumb the depths because we don't realize that it's filled with what the world offers instead of God.

On a hot afternoon many centuries after Isaac restored those wells, two people sat beside a similar one. Jesus met a woman there, who due to some poor life decisions that left her ostracized from her community, had to retrieve water alone. In this encounter, Jesus offers the woman not water that could sustain her for the rest of the day, but water that could sustain her for eternity: himself. This account from John 4 reminds us of the importance of clear, living water in our lives, water that sustains us and gives us our identity. Many of us have a false understanding of ourselves because we have allowed society, rather than God, to define who we are. The question "Who am I?" is much more interesting than "What do I do?' However, the fact remains that many of us are more comfortable with the latter question because we fear answering the first one.

For many years, it was difficult for me to relax. I remember spending the first four days of a seven-day vacation just unwinding from the stress I had wrapped around myself. As a pastor and seminary professor, I relished all God was allowing me to do. The busier I kept myself, the more I felt I was effective in ministry. "How many homebound people can I visit today?" "How much earlier can I get to the office than I did yesterday?" I was in competition with myself in the name of ministry. To be sure, motivating oneself is not detrimental to our spiritual well-being, for accountability is healthy for us. However, when we stay busy and motivate ourselves for the wrong reasons, our work is accomplished in our own name and not in Christ's name. What I knew about myself was through what I did, where I went, and what people thought about me. Perhaps this is precisely why that cruise vacation was the most relaxing one I had ever taken: the boat was always moving. In the words of Carl McColman, "We are so busy labeling ourselves, judging ourselves, categorizing and interpreting ourselves that we simply lack the time or energy to discover our deepest, truest identity."[2] We spend our energies on activities that don't have eternal significance and then wonder why our lives are filled with stress and exhaustion. We can't seem to find the time to explore the living well that is our soul.

The Importance of Self-Discovery

We are living a human existence unlike that of any generation that has gone before us. If you have lived in a home built before 1960, you may have discovered one of the reasons why our existence is different. My wife and I recently moved after fourteen years in the same home. It was exhausting trying to find the perfect place to live (which we finally concluded doesn't exist). We finally settled on a fifty-five-year-old home. It was in great condition and in a great neighborhood. The location, size, and price were right. However, we soon discovered a major implication of living in an older home: the size of the closets. When this home was built, all people needed were a few different outfits and a couple of pairs of shoes. You didn't need much closet space for that. Today, we personalize wardrobes so we won't ever be caught wearing what someone else is wearing. And how many colors of automobiles are around today? They used to come in just a few colors and with very few options. We might have the same smartphone, but we can personalize them to such an extent with cases, apps, and backgrounds that no one would ever mistake ours for theirs. We are the most personalized generation in history.

We seek this personalization in the externals of our lives, of course. We fail to realize that in the deep well of our lives, God has already created us unique and unrepeatable. Each of us is unique in all of creation, yet many of us live our lives as if we need to create our own uniqueness. God has already done that by making us one of a kind interiorly, where it matters. When the focus of our lives is predominantly exterior, we face three dilemmas. First, this approach affects our understanding of ourselves. We are not our hairstyle or waist size or skin color. We are not our wardrobe or our vehicle or our social status. We are much deeper than that: we are

2. McColman, *Befriending Silence*, 27.

defined by the internal well of our souls that God created before we were ever born. When we define ourselves by an external standard, we deceive ourselves and become foreigners to our very souls. Remember that we were created in the image and likeness of God. Since we can't see God, then the essence of who we are is unseen, as well.

Several years ago, a prominent NFL player realized it was time to retire. He held a press conference to make the announcement, and it was all the sports media reported for several days. However, about four months later, he held a second press conference and announced to the world that his retirement was over. He came back but did not play at his former level and retired for a second time after the next season. For his entire life, this player had been told that he was a football player. In many ways, that was how he identified himself. If he wasn't part of a team, he didn't know who he was. What we do is not who we are. Who we are is who we are.

Second, an external-only understanding of ourselves negatively affects our understanding of God. We begin to see God as a master who expects us to behave in a certain way and accomplish certain tasks in order to please him. We even fall into the trap of wanting God to be proud of us for how we live. Christians in the holiness tradition often succumb to this temptation: "If I act a certain way, avoid certain things, do this or that, then I am holy." This couldn't be further from a proper approach to Christian holiness! It's impossible to make ourselves holy. The work of the Holy Spirit in our lives does that. If we could make ourselves holy, or faithful, or righteous, then the work of Christ on the cross was for nothing and the indwelling of the Holy Spirit superfluous. Countless Christians have falsely believed that they can work themselves into God's favor. This is what led Martin Luther to depression. He believed he could work his way up to God, who after approving of Luther's good works, would then lower a divine hand and bring Luther to faith. Luther finally came to understand that it is by faith in Christ alone (an internal dimension) that we are saved by the grace of God. From that initial faith, we are led outside of ourselves to be the light of God in the world.

Maurice Néoncelle has a wonderful way of expressing how God's nature relates to human identity. "God is my originating principle, my absolute superior, who forever escapes me, from whom I can never escape."[3] To understand ourselves, we cannot begin to do so apart from knowing that we come from God and can never exist beyond the realm of God. This does not imply that God keeps us captive, for true love is freely chosen. First

---

3. Nédoncelle, *God's Encounter with Man*, 78.

John 4:16 states that God is love, and all who abide in love abide in God, and God abides in them. To understand ourselves apart from God is to have little understanding of ourselves at all.

The two incarnational natures of Jesus, divine and human, represent the nature of humanity. When we meditate on Jesus' human nature, we see in it the same beauty that we see in Jesus' divine nature.[4] Being of both equally, Jesus has both the divine authority and the human representation to serve as both our Lord and our Savior. I wonder if we overly complicate the nature of Jesus. In the famous words of Augustine, *Deus vere et summe simplex est* ("God is truly and supremely simple").[5] For Augustine, God is simple because God's identity is identical to God's attributes. Think about all the ways we overcomplicate not only our lives, but the way we understand ourselves. When Jesus described himself to his disciples in the Gospels, he did so without grandiose, complex language. He made statements about himself that may have confused the disciples at times, but his statements were straightforward and without complicated language. I can imagine Jesus using complicated theological language to describe his life and mission in heaven and on earth. Had he done that, however, he would have been filling his disciples with theological information. Instead, Jesus was most interested in their formation into his disciples and citizens of God's kingdom. Having a right understanding of who God is involves more than mental exercises of theological logic. It requires a heart malleable enough for the Holy Spirit to mold us into the people God the Father has created us to be. The more we know ourselves, the more we know God, and the more we know God, the more we know ourselves. "Lord, let me know myself, let me know You."[6] Christian thinkers have affirmed this double-knowledge of Augustine since the bishop of Hippo in the fourth century. In the wondrous, complex world in which we live, perhaps all we really need to know are these two.

A third danger of misunderstanding ourselves through an exterior-centric existence is that it makes us the god of our lives. If we lead with our actions and not out of response to God, we are simply placing our trust in ourselves rather than in Almighty God. This could be trust in our gifts, our skills, our church budgets, our leadership, our capacity as parents, or other things. When our trust is in anything other than God, it is pride; and pride

---

4. Chautard, *The Spirit of Simplicity*, 27.

5. Augustine, *On the Trinity*, IV:7.

6. Augustine, *Soliloquies*, II.1.

is the personalization of idolatry. Pride is the lowest common denominator in the realm of sin, for all sin originates with pride. Were it not for pride, Adam and Eve would not have sinned (Genesis 3). When David took a census of his armies to assess his capacity to defend the kingdom, he was condemned for his pride (2 Samuel 24). When the devil tempted Jesus in the wilderness, it included a temptation to appear great and powerful before others, which was pride (Matthew 4).

Knowing what tempts us is a blessing of self-understanding. What concerns us about what other people see in our lives is sometimes evidence of what is most important to us. If we're concerned with our looks, our status, our knowledge, or other external aspects of life, then materialism may be our great temptation. Conversely, if we're primarily concerned with how spiritual we look or how holy others think we are, then spiritual pride may be the great temptation of our lives. Whichever is the case, what's important is that we're honest with ourselves; and of course, self-honesty is only realized when we have a good idea of who we are as God has created us.

Colossians 3:17 states that as we live our lives, whatever we do should be done as a representative of the Lord Jesus Christ. This is the opposite of pride, for in this mind-set we are not living to represent ourselves or to make a good impression on people. We cannot live as Christ's representatives unless Christ has first transformed us. Again, our doing emerges from our being. To be a faithful follower of Jesus means that our internal affects our external, not the other way around. Yet as we have seen, unfortunately this is not always manifested in the lives of Christians or in local churches. Balancing the external and internal aspects of our lives provides opportunities for us to hear God's voice and transform the world around us. This provides us with a holistic experience of life.

The Whole Self

Increasingly, people around the world are taking ecotourism vacations. Visiting not tourist destinations, but natural wonders of the world, allows people to connect more deeply with the beauty of God's creation. One popular destination is, surprisingly, Antarctica or the polar ice caps. What tourists flock to see are the beautiful icebergs that have broken from the frozen land masses and are floating towards warmer climates. Icebergs are spectacular to behold—almost majestic in their size and strength. Yet what most people see is only 10 percent of the iceberg. Most of it is underwater, hidden from view. To board an iceberg tourist boat and take a picture of one of these mammoth frozen structures is not to take a picture of the iceberg, but just part of the iceberg.

The same principle could be applied in other ways, as well. Do you visit Paris, or just parts of Paris? I spent most of my growing years in New Orleans. I'm humored when I hear people say, "I went to New Orleans for a convention. I love that city." How can they know a city when they spent a few days in one small part of it? It's like looking at 10 percent of an iceberg and saying, "I saw an iceberg." Our lives are the same way. What people see is only part of who we are. We put forth an image of ourselves that we want to convey to the world, and hope people will believe that's who we are. The reality is that many of us know 10 percent of ourselves really well, but we don't completely know the other 90 percent that lies beneath the surface of our external lives. The implications of this lack of self-knowledge extend to our families and children, whom we raise to live almost exclusively in an external world, carefully crafting that family and personal image we want the world to see.

Recently I took an Amtrak train across the central part of the United States. I felt the wonder of a child as I swayed back and forth in my small sleeper car and the train clicked down the tracks. Field after field whirred by my window and I looked at trees and ponds that were always there, yet for me, they were new and exciting. As we sped through some small towns and stopped in others, I discovered communities whose names I have never heard. Yet for some people, these small, aging towns were the only place they had ever called home. As I watched them in their townships, I wondered if their identity and worth were based on their small-town isolation. Did they feel trapped in these little towns? Did they have the financial means to move away and start anew? Had they been able to discover more of this phenomenal world than just the few acres of their communities? My journey on the train taught me that the world is much bigger than I knew that it was, and I have been blessed to explore many parts of this world. We think we know more than we really do about the world because we can see it online, yet that knowledge of the world is limited. When we frame our identity on a vocation, an address, a surname, a nation, or even a denomination, we limit our capacity to understand ourselves holistically. We are more than our actions. We are more than our successes or failures. We are more than where we live or what we do.

In 1 Samuel 15, we find Saul, the first king of Israel, having just defeated an enemy in battle. Although Saul had instructions not to spare anyone or anything in the evil nation they defeated, he kept the flocks of sheep and goats to distribute to the people of Israel, and he spared the king of that nation to use as a trophy, showing everyone the results of his victorious battle. When he returned home to victory celebrations, the prophet Samuel confronted the king. "Although you're small in your eyes, are you not still the head of the tribes of Israel?" Samuel knew that what was important for Saul was what people saw. If he had a more holistic understanding of himself, he would not have been so concerned with his external reputation. Because Saul had developed only the external nature of who he was and was therefore unable to serve God faithfully, he was removed as king.

We Are More Than We Think We Are

Perhaps, like Saul, many of us fall into this trap because we don't really understand what it means to be human. Too many times we equate the word *spirituality* with emotions. Certainly our spirituality has an effect on our emotions, and our emotions can have an effect on our spirituality, but they are not one and the same. What are emotions? How do they interact with our spiritual nature? In the middle ages, Thomas Aquinas, following the model set forth centuries earlier by Greek philosopher Aristotle, presents a hierarchical order of creation known as "The Great Chain of Being."[7] Simplified, the order of creation can be viewed this way:

> Angels/Heavenly Beings
> Humans
> ----------------
> Animals
> Plants
> Rocks/Earth

What this list demonstrates is that angels and humans are above the rest of creation because in all of creation, only angels and humans can have a relationship with God. As Psalm 8 states, "You've created people just a little lower than the angels." That's a magnanimous statement from King David. In a single line in a Psalm about the majesty of God, David presents the general nature of humanity in a deeply profound way. If we

---

7. Aquinas, *Summa Theologica*, I, q. 2, a. 3, ad 2.

understood the gravity of that description, our view of ourselves would not be limited to our life on earth. As much as we love our puppies and kittens, the reality is the Bible never says anything about them having a relationship with God. Unlike the rest of creation, human beings were created by God to be spiritual beings. It's part of who we are. We were created to have a relationship with God. When we ignore this aspect of our lives, we fail to live a completely human existence.

Some of us are uncomfortable with the thought of self-discovery. Perhaps we've been conditioned by society or even by well-meaning Christians that the means to faithfulness is through our work. Perhaps the thought of self-discovery means digging up buried hurts we would like to keep submerged in our lives. Others may fear a search for true identity because thy are afraid of what they might discover about themselves. If we have given our lives to Christ, and asked him to transform all of our lives, that means *all* of our lives; even the hurts and biases and disappointments we do not even realize exist. No matter how deeply these things are buried in our lives, they affect who we are. A clean house with closets that hide the clutter is not a clean house.

Self-discovery is the first degree of prayer because after we make acquaintances with our true selves, we can approach God honestly. Our internal life is that deep well of the soul that cuts through the soil, the sand, the bedrock, and all the way down to that refreshing, life-giving water at the bottom. This is where we can truly encounter Christ, and Christ can introduce us to ourselves, perhaps for the first time. It's this muck of living a purely external life that spoils the water of our souls and our opportunity to experience self-discovery. Just as Isaac had to re-dig the wells that the Philistines had filled with sand, in God's perfect timing we realize it is time to give God the shovel so God can dig the sludge out of the well of our heart.

God identifying himself to Moses as "I Am Who I Am" is revealing. God could have identified himself as "I Do What I Do," but that wouldn't be quite right. Certainly, God has done and continues to do many wonderful things: God created the universe and all we need to survive. God created you and me. God the Father sent Jesus, God the Son, to give himself unto death for our sins and sent God the Holy Spirit to empower us and remain with and in us. God heals us, hears our prayers, gives us insight and wisdom, and does countless more things that we overlook every day. Yet all this "doing" actually sprouts from God's "being." What God does is a natural outflow from who God is: God is love.

Western society clamors for our attention with the latest products and newest styles of every imaginable item we can buy. Streaming television services provide hundreds of channels for us to spend hours each day watching. The Internet brings the world into our homes and into the palms of our hands. Unlike Jesus' words to the disciples in Matthew 10:9 not to worry about money, clothes, or what we need when we go about in society representing him, Christians by the millions spend countless dollars purchasing all the items we *think* we need. Pastors are not immune, either—in order to preach on Sunday morning, we have to have the latest computer tablet for our sermon notes and the newest model cell phone so people can reach us if they need us. Yes, we live in an external world.

The *imago Dei*

Society tells us (even society in the body of Christ) that *doing* fosters *being*. This could not be more false, because that mind-set turns us into victims of our activities. A proper understanding of ourselves occurs when who we are guides how we spend our time. Since we are created in the image of God (*imago Dei*), then like God, the nature of our being is a noun, not a verb. There are more instances in Scripture about who God is ("God is light," "God is my helper," etc.) than there are about what God has done. Yet both are there, for what God does is important and necessary. Since we're created in the *imago Dei*, the essence of what it means to be human is like God in that respect: our doing (external life) flows from our being (internal life). The "I" of our identity is an eye into our soul. If we earnestly desire to know ourselves well, we must not fear the "I" or the "eye."

In her insightful 1958 book *The Human Condition*, Jewish author Hannah Arendt writes that our lives have two dimensions, the *vita activa*, or the "active life," and the *vita contemplativa*, or the "contemplative life."[8] It's the development of these two facets of our lives in equal portions that helps us live as complete human beings. The external (active) life is about what we do in the lives of people and in the world. The internal (spiritual) life is about who we are inside of ourselves. For us to live faithfully and effectively for God, our external life must sprout from our internal life. If we do not have a rich understanding of our spiritual life, we fail to see the

---

8. Arendt, *The Human Condition*, 318. While Arendt was not a professing Christian, her work with Augustine's understanding of love remains important in the study of the human condition.

richness of the person God created us to be. Perhaps we see ourselves as we see the ocean from a boat. Although it takes some courage and faith to get there, it's much more rewarding to see ourselves from beneath the waves.

If we are not careful, a life focused on our internal self can lead to self-absorption and pride. Bernard of Clairvaux wrote that any internal endeavor (knowledge, spiritual growth, self-understanding, etc.) that does not result in love for others is nothing but a selfish pursuit.[9] We don't exist for ourselves, but for others. Our external activities are the manifestation of our internal discoveries about ourselves and God. I believe it is that aspect of self-understanding that is so very important in our relationship with God and in our capacity to engage God in prayer. When we meet someone, we can be tempted to make a good impression by inflating ourselves, our status, our friends, and other aspects of our lives. When we do this, we are introducing ourselves as someone we are not, which is actually disrespecting the person we meet because we do not respect him or her enough to present ourselves for who we really are. Other times, we want to impress our neighbors by having the best landscaping, the nicest car, or the perfect family. People think they know us, but they only know what we want them to see. We become a living social media profile—only presenting to the world that which we are comfortable sharing—which in many instances is far from the reality of who we really are.

Knowing how to describe our relationship with God can be beneficial in understanding ourselves, particularly when the events of life suddenly take a turn we did not expect. I write this during a global pandemic from COVID-19, in which people around the world have been forced to isolate themselves from others. As a professor, my pedagogical routine has been upended. As a father, our daughter's wedding has had to be completely transformed and transitioned from a large celebration with her friends to a small family event. Families around the world have been forced to spend time together, sequestered in their homes. I do not believe it is a coincidence that pockets of frustration and anger are popping up around the world. Trapped in abnormal routines, individuals and families are faced with gazing into a giant mirror. Now that our lives are unpredictable and outside of our normal routines, each of us has an opportunity to take a long, deep look at ourselves. It's as if we have woken to a strange world in which we can no longer place our identities in our daily routines and tasks. For some of us, this creates chaos, as we are not the person we thought we were. However,

---

9. Bernard, Sermon XXXVI, *Sermons on the Song of Songs.*

if we approach this new way of life with a different perspective, it could be a season of deep, personal discovery—a real blessing from God.

The Pursuit of Authentic Existence

Our relationship with God is the same way. We should approach God honestly, without attempting to present ourselves to God in a way that doesn't represent ourselves. Certainly we don't need to introduce ourselves to God! After all, we're created in God's image and likeness (Genesis 1:26). God will always know us better than we know ourselves, for the core of our identity is hidden in God. In fact, the prayers we pray to God are already within him.[10] Why, then, do we sometimes feel as though we need to impress God? We may begin an intensive Bible reading program, volunteer at our local church, or commit to praying for an hour each day; all just so God will be proud of us—and approve of us, even if we have no desire to do these things. Knowing ourselves well—and being honest with ourselves—is imperative if we are to grow in our prayer life with God. Jesus tells us we're to love God with all our heart and mind and soul (Matthew 22:37). We cannot do that authentically if we don't have a healthy understanding of ourselves.

Many Christian writers throughout the past two millennia have stressed the need for self-discovery as a means to intimacy with God. It is important for us to deal with issues from our past that cloud our understanding of God for who God really is. Understanding ourselves is comprehending and developing both our internal and external lives as God created us. Many times, as we grow in Christlikeness; God reveals to us aspects of ourselves that we never had the courage to see. Remember: Growth in grace is not prescriptive. In the spiritual life, two plus two doesn't always equal four, and sequential steps aren't necessarily in the right order. Sometimes our growth in self-understanding and our growth in our love for Christ happen at the same time.

John Wesley, the founder of Methodism, lived an extremely active life. He traveled by horseback all across the nation, preaching thousands of sermons. He established and oversaw Methodist lay preachers. He wrote extensively, including a detailed journal that spanned several decades. He organized ministries for the poor. Later in life, he commissioned missionaries to evangelize North America. Yet in all of this doing, in all of this external activity, he rose each morning before sunrise to spend a

---

10. Nédoncelle, *God's Encounter with Man*, 78.

considerable amount of time in prayer. All the things he did in the name of Christ were in response to who he was in Christ. That was his desire for those in the Methodist movement: that personal holiness would lead to social holiness. Social holiness (our relationships with others) should always sprout from personal holiness (our relationship with Christ). This is the essence of what it means to be a disciple of Jesus. Because we have given our true selves to God, we can offer our transformed selves to the world. Since a life in Christ means that Christ becomes our life (Colossians 3:4), we are able to offer the world not ourselves, but Jesus himself.

Michael Casey has written that authentic prayer grows out of authentic living: "At some stage in our life we have to make the transition from being 'good' to being ourselves."[11] Casey does not suggest that our moral character has no meaning or purpose. Rather, he encourages us to stop trying to do the right things and simply live out of who we are as God has created us. When we strive to live the right way, do or don't do certain things, or try to please God with our spiritual activities, we've taken our focus off of God and placed it onto ourselves. It's like the person who needs to lose weight who focuses on what he should or should not eat. His focus should be on overall healthy living instead of on the minutiae of how many French fries he should consume at once. When we see ourselves as beloved people created in the image and likeness of God, and when we have been adopted as children of God through Christ, not only do we see ourselves differently; we live with a holy authenticity that is not a burden or obligation, but a joy.

Self-knowledge involves a surrender of the will. When can see ourselves with a divine reality, we realize how desperately we need God. I've grieved for people I've met throughout the years of life and ministry who said they didn't need to rely on God because God gave them everything they need to make it on their own. When I hear people say this, they're giving me clues that they are lost to themselves, for if they knew their true identity, they would recognize their absolute need for God. In Matthew 16:24, Jesus tells his disciples that if they want to be his disciple, they need to deny themselves, take up their cross, and follow him. Knowing ourselves is not the opposite of denying ourselves. In fact, it may be impossible to deny ourselves if we do not first know who we are. How do we surrender our lives when we don't know what life we have to surrender? Similarly, how do we take up our cross and follow Jesus if we don't know which cross has our name on it? To be a disciple of Jesus is possible only when we know

11. Casey, *Grace on the Journey to God*, 88.

ourselves so well that we are willing to surrender ourselves to the love and providence of God.

Approaching God from the authentic self affords us the freedom to commune with God without fear or shame. We come to God as we are, without regard for our educational or professional achievement, our social status, our degree of holiness, or even without our commitment to God. By peeling away the layers of our lives that the world claims is part of our identity, we come to God humbly, as a child who is not yet soured by the sarcastic attitudes so common in mature adults. John Chrysostom preached that when a person comes to God without the ornamentation of the world, that person's soul is able "to give itself entirely to itself, and to devote all its attention to becoming beautiful and precious in the sight of God."[12] This healthy, vulnerable, stripped-down understanding of ourselves allows us to see that we are in need of God. This leads us to engaging with God in authentic prayer.

Perhaps the image of stripping ourselves of mature adulthood and returning to the worldview of a child is a wonderful way of exploring this first degree of prayer. Children have no issues presenting themselves as they really are. If they feel like crying, they cry. If they have something to say, they will say it. They know how helpless they are in the world, so they look to adults for security and guidance. For several years I served as a pastor to children, even leading a children's worship service that contained all the elements of adult worship, but in a way children could understand. We prayed for countless sick dogs, cats, and fish. My preaching style was primarily narrative, with plenty of modern parables. However, when these children sang modern hymns and other spiritual songs, I have no doubt they believed every word of the lyrics. If I played the wrong chord on my guitar, they did not even notice—or care. What mattered to them was that I was spending time with them, playing my guitar for God. During the Scripture-reading time, it was common for a child to respond with an audible gasp: "Woah!" Their capacity to see themselves, their world, and God was concrete and real.

When we approach God in prayer, may we never forget to do so as a child. Children do not worry about proper vocabulary in their prayers or being theologically precise. They simply share their lives with God. As Jesus said to his disciples in Mark 10, we must receive the kingdom of God like a child in order to enter it. When we approach God with our authentic

12. Chrysostom, *Homilies*, 83.

self—like a child—Jesus invites us to himself, takes us into his arms, and blesses us. This is the essence of the first degree of prayer. Self-discovery, or rediscovery, becomes a joy since are freed to approach God initially with childlike faith rather than with academic logic and theological precision. Reasoned logic and sound theology have an important role in Christian faith, but they are not the essence of who we are in Christ. As God is love, so are we. This realization is prayer in the first degree.

3

Conversation with God
(Prayer in the Second Degree)

THE AIR IN THE rainforest around me was so thick I felt the need to push it away as I hiked. The floor of the dark, thick forest, covered with ferns, moss, and fallen fir trees, made me thankful for the person who labored on my behalf to carve my little path. It was only 40 degrees outside, yet my shirt was soaked with perspiration as made our way up the steep trail. My friend and I walked around a tall Douglas fir and immediately noticed the density of the forest was beginning to thin. A clearing was ahead, and for the first time that day, we saw blue sky. Enthroned behind the open meadow of blooming wildflowers, in all its 14,410-foot glory, was the active composite volcano known to the Salish people as Tahoma and to the rest of us as Mt. Rainier. I had never seen anything so massive and majestic. I stopped, sat down on a fallen tree, and stared in disbelief at the sight before me. My reaction must have made an impression on my friend, who reminded me, "And that's just one side of it."

I hope we never lose the wonder of this world God created. From mountain magnificence, to the intricacy of a microscopic organism, to the glance across the room between friends, to the deep love shared by a couple on their fiftieth anniversary, to a bowl of soup placed in the thin hands of the hungry or the bread and wine offered to a kneeling disciple, the number of extraordinary events this world has to offer are beyond our capacity to count. Yet no experience, relationship, or natural vista comes even close to comparing with the phenomenon that is a simple prayer offered to God. That we're able to communicate with the omniscient, omnipresent, and omnipotent triune God of holy love and grace is beyond our capacity to process.

The Purpose of Prayer

In prayer, our thoughts and words do not merely vanish into nothingness. They transcend the entirety of the world we know and travel straight into the heart of God. In some sense, this mystery of prayer is unfathomable. How do we know with absolute certainty that not only does God hear our prayers, but also that God responds to our prayers? It requires faith, which itself requires inexplicable trust. All of this mystery, uncertainty, faith, and trust are actually a cumulative blessing, for if humanity could understand the complexities involved in prayer, then God would not be great enough to be worthy of hearing and answering our prayers.

I have a hunch that for many Christians, the act of prayer is something we know we need to do, but we don't. We might tell someone we will be praying for them, but in the end, we either forget or engage in quick thoughts of goodwill for them. Over the years, people (including seminary students) have shared with me that they're intimidated by prayer. Perhaps we don't want to embarrass ourselves by praying the wrong thing, praying in a way that is not theologically sound, or getting so distracted in a prayer that we feel like we have disappointed God. The reality of prayer is that just as we might die physically without the ability to breathe fresh air, without prayer in our lives, our souls wither away into self-absorption and despair. To exist in the world as a human being, prayer is essential for life. It matters not if we pray the right way. What matters is that we pray. To paraphrase a friend of mine, times of prayer are ovens where the spiritual bread is baked. In prayer, we acknowledge that we are not the end of our lives; we need Someone greater than ourselves, even if we don't have a full understanding of who that Someone is. French philosopher Maurice Nédoncelle calls this admission of a need for prayer "an avowal of inadequacy."[1] God has gifted humans with the capacity to do many things. However, to be truly human is to acknowledge the impoverished nature of our being. We become aware of the frailty of the human condition without God. When we know ourselves, we know that we can approach God because we were created to be in relationship with an approachable, loving God.

---

1. Nédoncelle, *God's Encounter with Man*, 29.

Prayer compels us to acknowledge (either implicitly or explicitly) that all we experience with our five senses is not the whole of this world. Prayer is a recognition that we are not capable of managing our lives on our own. It is an admission of our human frailty to control every aspect of our lives. Prayer in this basic sense involves trust beyond our control. Like a child who knows that food, shelter, and clothes must come from an adult in her life, so we know in prayer that what we need comes from God. In our times of distress, we often turn to God, who we know is greater than our distress —even if we do not yet have a relationship with God—in the hope that God will hear us. Even the atheist facing a critical life experience will turn to a god. This deity may be critical thinking, financial security, advancements in medicine, or even the escape into alcohol or other numbing agents. In this sense, atheism cannot exist, for those who refuse to believe in an omniscient God instead place their trust in themselves or in their experiences, which in turn become the deities in their lives.

God uses prayer to reveal to us the areas in our lives where we've refused to submit. In his sixth sermon on Jesus's Sermon on the Mount, John Wesley reminds us that "our prayers are the proper test of our desires . . . What we may not pray for, neither should we desire."[2] Prayers illumine the places in our hearts we want to keep hidden from God. In prayer, the Holy Spirit invites us to acknowledge that our deepest yearnings are not as desirable for us as we imagine them to be. This wisdom from Wesley became realized when Patrick came to the pastor's study to meet with me. Patrick was in his mid-thirties, married, and had two adorable children. He was a leader in the congregation and others trusted him. His insurance business was booming. By the look on his face when I handed him a cup of coffee, however, I knew something was awry. He shared with me that his life was missing something. It was as if he had a puzzle piece missing. After listening to him share and asking him some pointed questions about his relationship with Christ, he finally shared what was wrong: "My neighbor got a new Corvette last week and I'm furious. I'm the one who told him I've always wanted one but that I couldn't afford it." I asked Patrick if he thought about asking God to give him a Corvette. "Seriously?" he asked. "The preacher is asking me to pray for a Corvette?" I did not have to say another word, for a simple wink was all I had to do to respond. He was desiring something that he would never ask God to give him. As he stood up to leave, he said, "I think I'm going to go home and wash my Buick."

2. Wesley, Sermon XXVI, 332.

Asking God for the desires of our heart is what Jesus tells us to do. When Jesus says, "Ask and it will be given to you; seek and you will find; knock and the door will be open to you," we must be careful about our request to God, as what we desire may not be what is best for us. A progression exists in this word from Jesus. Asking requires the least amount of commitment from us, as we're just at the stage of inquiry. Seeking necessitates a commitment of energy, time, and perseverance. If what we are seeking is worth it, we will keep seeking. Knocking is the most difficult for us, for when we knock on a door, we expect the person behind the door to engage us. Knocking in prayer requires the deepest commitment of the three, for in a moment, we will be face to face with the master of the home. When we ask and seek the Lord, but are hesitant to knock, we resist ministry from the Holy Spirit. In fact, Wesley said the neglect of knocking is a great hindrance to Christian holiness because we refuse to invite the Holy Spirit to occupy our lives.[3]

The Reality of Prayer

One reality about prayer is that it is impossible for us to begin a conversation with God, for God is always in conversation with us. Many times, we do not hear God because our focus is elsewhere. The aspect of God's grace that always goes before us is highlighted in Bernard's first sermon on the Advent season. Bernard writes with amazement that God would be the one who would first come to us, for we are the people in need. Normally, he writes, those in need go to the person who can help them. God certainly does not need us, yet God comes to us before our hearts and souls have any recognition of need.[4] Before our cognizant awareness of a need, God already knows that need and has been ministering to us in the background of our lives; waiting patiently for us to reach out to him. This Divine, prevenient action in our lives is yet another example of God's deep love for us. Rather than wanting something from us in return for God's action in our lives, God's love for us is completely selfless. God doesn't need our love in return but knows that our love for Him is the silent longing of our lives.

Prayer in the second degree is a simple realization that since we understand ourselves as being created in God's image and likeness, we need God. This awareness drives us out of ourselves to focus our thoughts and hearts

3. See Wesley's Sermon XXX, 401.
4. Bernard, *Sermons for Advent*, Sermon 1.8.

on God. The most simple prayer we can pray is, "God, help!" While this might seem like a selfish prayer, it is actually a soul crying out to God in a helpless state. I have prayed this prayer more than once as I've stepped into a congregational pulpit to share a homily or to preach a sermon in a seminary chapel filled with biblical scholars and theologians. Similarly, as I was being rolled into the operating room for risky and delicate cancer surgery, the last thing I remember seeing was a crucifix attached to the wall of the operating room. It prompted me to ask God to guide the surgeon's divinely created hands. Self-directed prayers are scattered throughout Scripture. From Moses at the burning bush (Exodus 4:13), to Psalms of help (e.g., Psalms 31, 86, 143), to Elijah on Mt. Horeb (1 Kings 19:10), to Jesus in the garden on the night of his arrest (Matthew 26:39), to Paul asking the Lord to remove some sort of unknown struggle in his life (2 Corinthians 12:7), the great people of faith in the Bible understood the necessity of praying seemingly simple, self-directed prayers in times of need.

Another major aspect of prayer in the second degree is our intercession for others. This can manifest itself both personally and corporately. When we place our own needs behind us to pray for someone else, we step between that individual and God to intercede on their behalf. Richard Foster correctly sees prayers of intercession as the priestly ministry of all believers.[5] Just as the priests of Israel went before God on behalf of all the people, all Christians have the task of going before the most high God on behalf of others. This is the duty of all Christ-followers; it is not optional or just for those called to prayer ministries. When we pray for others, we are forsaking our own needs to focus our soul's energy on God's intervention in someone else's life. Not only is this scriptural (see Luke 23:34 or James 5:16), it's a sign of love for someone else, even if they never know of our love for them.

Intercessory prayer is an example of the interconnectedness of those in the body of Christ. When we pray for others, we enter acts of intercession that are already taking place in heaven. Our prayers join with the Holy Trinity and the community of heaven that are already underway. In the eloquent words of Douglas Steere, our souls "are interconnected in God, as though the many wicks of our lamps draw their oil from the same full cruse in which they are all immersed."[6] The reality of this interconnectedness in the kingdom of God in intercessory prayer extends to all aspects of life. Just

5. Foster, *Prayer*, 191.

6. Steere, *Dimensions of Prayer*, 82.

as the Holy Trinity is One God in a loving relationship between the Father, the Son, and the Holy Spirit, we are called to live in unified community of holy love with one another (John 17:21). We need others to pray for us. They need us to pray for them. This one aspect of life in the body of Christ sustains us and reminds us that much of the work of the church is that which goes unseen.

Many of us do not value the gift of prayerful intercession from others. Perhaps the phrase "I'll be praying for you" has become nothing more to us than a polite way to end a Christian conversation. J. Ellsworth Kalas, a former president of Asbury Theological Seminary, was known for his world-class Bible exposition and narrative preaching, for his warm, grandfatherly voice, and for his theologically down-to-earth practical wisdom. To me, he will always be the man of God who sent me a handwritten note letting me know that he prayed for me at a certain time on a specific day. I remember feeling a bit bewildered that week. I had received some crushing news I was not expecting, and I began to question my very call to ministry. Knowing that he took the time to lift me before God in the throne room of heaven made me feel loved and cherished when I felt neither on that day.

One Person's Story

When I was ten years old, my pastor told me in a blunt way that God had called me to be a pastor. Honestly, being a pastor was the last thing on the mind of this insecure fifth grader. As I grew, to describe me as socially awkward would be kind. Because I was focused on myself and constantly compared myself with others, I had a deep sense of inferiority. I developed a speech stammer, shied away from athletics, and withdrew into socially isolating activities, such as reading, writing, and photography. In college, I became a summer camp counselor because interacting with children was not intimidating to me. That I would meet the woman of my dreams at that camp was evidence to me that I had at least some worth. When I graduated from college with a degree in professional writing, I went to Rev. Dick Freeman, our pastor at First United Methodist in Waco, Texas to ask if he could help me find a position in town. We had joined this large congregation just a few months before, and the pastor did not really know us. He replied, "You're going to seminary because God has called you to ministry. Then you'll come back here and be my associate pastor." Once again, God was showing his grace to me, even though I couldn't fathom ministry as a pastor.

In seminary, it was no surprise to anyone that I put off enrolling in the required preaching class as long as I could. Once in class, I signed up for the very last date of student sermon presentations. It was on this occasion that the power of intercessory prayer became real in my life, and in an unexpected way. Due to my stuttering insecurities, I was sure my ten-minute homily on Psalm 121 would extend to twenty minutes. As I stepped into the pulpit in the preaching classroom, I noticed a group of classmates huddled in the back of the room in prayer. Others filtered over to them until the entire class had joined the prayer group. I thought this was curious, but I needed to begin because the light on the camera connected to the VCR was blinking impatiently at me. I opened my mouth to speak and I have not stuttered since. In that moment, God instantaneously delivered me from a life of insecurity and gave me the insight to know that any weakness I might have is nothing compared to the strength of God.

When the Psalm 121 homily was over, my fellow students were still in prayer. My professor said, "I can't talk about this now," and left the classroom. Not knowing what to do or where to go, I decided to join my classmates in the corner of the room. Yes, I was delivered from stuttering; but even more than that, I became aware of the intrinsic value of the selfless holy love shared by those in the Christian community, especially when we take the time to pray for one another. Most of the time, God's response to us in his perfect will is implicit. Because we live in a world of information and knowledge, this can frustrate us. However, in this one instance in 1992, God was explicitly clear in his faithfulness. Today, I often teach classes on prayer to students in that very classroom. As these seminary students sit before me, I am acutely aware that all those years ago, when my peers stood in the gap between myself and God in the back of the room, and God replied to their intercession in ways far beyond their requests that day.

Pray So That God May Be Glorified

Not every request we bring before the Lord is answered the way we desire. If Jesus says in John 14:13, "Ask for anything in my name and I will give it to you," why doesn't this happen?" First of all, anything that we can ask in Jesus' name will be granted. Jesus' words are quite clear! However, the phrase "in my name" doesn't mean we can just utter the words "I pray this in Jesus' name." These aren't magic words that force God to do what we want God to do. Instead, praying in Jesus' name means praying and working as

Christ's representatives in the same heart and mind in which Jesus prayed and worked. We must not forget that Jesus in the garden of Gethsemane prayed, "Not my will, but yours be done." Praying for any reason other than to pray and work as Christ's representatives in order for God to be glorified is left out of this promise from Jesus. So why, then, doesn't God heal everyone when we pray, even if it's so that God might be glorified through the healing?

Certainly God is glorified through miraculous healing. However, God can also be glorified through our suffering. Physical suffering was a part of life for the first generations of Christians. They were imprisoned, beaten, starved, and put to death for their allegiance to Christ. The witness of people enduring years of pain yet rejoicing in God's faithfulness brings glory to the Almighty. Of course, we must remember the Apostle Paul himself, who testifies in 2 Corinthians 12:7–10 that on three different occasions he pleaded to the Lord to remove "a thorn in [his] flesh." Yet God said to Paul, "My grace is all you need. My power works best in weakness." Paul, who wrote more of the New Testament than any other person, who evangelized the Roman world, testifies that the Lord didn't heal him of this mysterious ailment. Yet God was glorified in not freeing Paul from it. When we think about it, God being glorified—lifted up as great to the world—is all that should matter in our lives.

In a letter to a Christian disciple known as "Miss Bishop," John Wesley celebrates the blessing of intercessory prayer. He writes, "If you . . . would do more for [someone] at my request than otherwise you would have done, how much more will God, at the request of his beloved children, give blessing to those they pray for, which otherwise he would not have given!"[7] In prayer, we do not change the mind of God. Instead, God invites us to participate with him. Because God became one of us in Jesus, and because the Holy Spirit resides in us, prayer is incarnational cooperation with God. We shouldn't shy away from this thought of cooperating with God. As sixth-century Desert Father Dorotheos of Gaza, wrote, "When God created [humanity], he breathed into [us] something divine, as it were a hot and bright spark added to reason . . ."[8] God did not breathe godly divinity into us, Dorotheos reminds us. Instead, it was a little bit of God's self. When sin entered the human heart, that divine spark was covered with the muck of depravity, but the image of God in us remained. This is why God hears the

7. Wesley, Letter DCCIX, "To Miss Bishop," 32.
8. Dorotheos, *Discourses and Sayings*, 104.

33

prayers of both the holy and the hateful, and this is why in prayer, especially for those who have the indwelling of the Holy Spirit in their souls, God invites us to participate with him.

God always answers our prayers in ways that are tailored to God's perfect, providential will. When God's perfect will conflicts with our imperfect will, how we respond indicates whether or not we are open to the Holy Spirit. In that moment, the Paraclete offers us an opportunity in to deepen our love for God. The issue in prayer is not what we necessarily desire, but what God desires for us. What matters is that we take our concerns to God. Some people drive themselves to anxious despair, never wanting to make a decision outside of God's will. Ultimately, God's will is that we are holy. As we ask God for a specific request, we should ask ourselves, "Would the granting of this request affect the holiness of my life?" The love God has for us is too profound and mysterious to grant us something that would drive us away from God.

Jesus' Instructions about Prayer

Three times in three verses of Matthew 6, Jesus makes the same assumption. In verses 5–7, as he is teaching the masses about prayer, Jesus says, "when you pray . . ." Jesus doesn't tell them they *should* pray. He assumes that prayer is already part of their lives. In these assumptions, Jesus lays a formative foundation for prayer. Prayer should not call attention to the one praying, and it should not be mindless thoughts recited over and over, trying to manipulate God with the right words. Instead, he reminds us that God the Father already knows what we need before we ask. For some of us, the thought of praying produces stress because we want to say the right words.

The reality is that God simply wants to hear from us. In what follows in verses 9–13, prayers of petition comprise a majority of what Jesus presents as a model for prayer. Foremost in this prayer is the person to whom prayer should be addressed: Our Father in heaven. A thin line exists between addressing the creator and ruler of the universe who has adopted us as his daughters and sons and mindlessly reciting familiar prayers in a ritualistic manner. Prayers of petition have nothing in common with mindless, recitational prayers. Bringing a petition before God is sharing the longings of the heart with God. When we recite prayers over and over, the result can be that we're trying to manipulate God into giving us what we desire. It's no different than a child begging a parent for a candy bar at the market: "Please, please, pleeeeeease!," trying to wear down the parent until she concedes. This is different from the persistent widow in Jesus' parable found in Luke 18:1–8, who pleads unwaveringly with her heart's desire.

God on Trial

Sometimes these prayers in the second degree look far different from heartfelt expressions for divine help or in our love for others. Often, our prayers involve addressing God with anger and frustration. In chapter 12 of Jeremiah, we find the prophet frustrated with God. It was God who had told Jeremiah that he had known him before Jeremiah was ever formed in his mother's womb. God had set him apart from others to serve as God's prophet to warn the people of their sin and encourage them to return to faithfulness in God. Jeremiah had accepted this responsibility, even though he knew life would not be easy for him. He may not have realized, however, just how difficult that life would be. When Jeremiah heard of a plot on his life, he became disheartened. When he discovered it was his own family that wanted to have him killed, it was all Jeremiah could take.

Jeremiah charges God with a crime and takes God to a mock court. He wants God to answer why those who are up to no good prosper and thrive. When God knows that they say the right things about God even though God is nowhere near their hearts, why does the Lord allow them to grow and produce fruit? They have the perfect godly smile, everyone seems to listen to them for their wisdom, but it is all show. Jeremiah, conversely, has committed himself to God. He has sacrificed everything, including his reputation, to follow God. The result is that no one listens to him, he has no followers, and his own father and brothers are out to kill him. In verse 3, Jeremiah invites God to examine him and test his heart. God knows that Jeremiah is faithful to his very core. Yet why do the wicked prosper while the faithful suffer? The prophet has put forth a solid case. How would God reply?

God's response was probably not what Jeremiah expected. In verse 5, God basically states, "Jeremiah, if you think it's bad now, just wait. It's going to get worse. If you can't handle this, how are you going to respond when the persecution really comes?" Jeremiah's lawsuit against God was actually a case against himself, for his eyes were on the situation of others and no on the faithfulness of his own life. Jesus would address this same topic hundreds of years later when he referred to those who focus on the faults of others rather than addressing their own issues (Matthew 7:1–5).

Jeremiah's faith in God was deep enough for him to keep trusting God when life did not go as he had planned. Rather than giving up on God, Jeremiah approached God in frustration and perhaps a bit of anger; but the fact that he still addressed God in prayer exhibits a healthy understanding of himself and of God. These characteristics of Jeremiah are what make him one of the most authentic people in Scripture, and a role model to us in what deep faith and trust in God look like in the real world of life and ministry.

The Perpetual Sufferer

Prayer in the second degree is our capacity to address God with our requests, petitions, intercessions, and like Jeremiah, our complaints. Implicit in this degree of prayer are potential obstacles to our relationship with God. The first impediment some may discover is a perpetual sufferer mentality, which ultimately is a lack of hope. Tomáš Halík reminds us that perpetual "indictments of God" can lead one to distrust God, which ultimately leads one away from God.[9] When our sole focus is the elimination of social injustice, for example, our gaze is not on a God worthy of trust, for a fallen world will always have unjust situations. Jesus tells us as much in Matthew 10:22 when he says that people of faith will always find bias against them. The early Christian martyrs in the Roman Empire understood that deadly persecution was always possible; their commitment to Christ made it a reality. They didn't try to influence the Roman Senate to pass laws that would alleviate the crimes against their sisters and brothers in the faith. Instead, the injustice against them caused their gaze to turn upward. Similarly, and despite our best efforts, some people will always live in poverty, desperately needing our help (Mark 14:7). Scripture is clear that the plight of the poor is our plight and we have an obligation to stand with them (Proverbs 31:8–9). The reason Benedict's *Rule* includes a chapter on the spiritual benefits of manual labor is to remind us that when we sweat in the open sun, we're identifying with the poor who have no other option in life.

A few years ago, I had a seminary student from a nation in Africa suffering from violent, religious turmoil. The Christians in the city where he served as a pastor were experiencing periodic violent attacks against them

9. Halík, *Patience with God*, 105.

by terrorists. One week, he came to me with the news that a small bomb had destroyed part of his congregation's church building. His people were helpless, as the local authorities did nothing to support them. I expressed to him my sorrow and asked if I could pray for the safety of his people. "NO!" he exclaimed. "I beg you not to pray for our safety. I ask that you pray that we will be courageous to stand for the truth of the gospel of Christ." He had an Acts 4 understanding of Christian persecution. This African brother had an eternal perspective of life. Raising a petition to God is almost always appropriate. Having the discernment to know how to make that petition demonstrates a deep sense of trust in the eschatological victory of God.

When Prayer Becomes Immobile

A second temptation in this degree of prayer is to remain stagnant in this type of communication with God. When this happens, prayer can evolve into a form of spiritual therapy. Millions of people have utilized therapists for emotional and psychological healing. I'm thankful for their gifts and calling. However, when we use prayer as a means to a spiritual end, we step close to the edge of using God for personal gain. I cannot count the number of times people have come to me and shared that they started having daily prayer, but stopped because they didn't seem to discern any benefit from it. Their prayer life withered on the vine of Christ because their prayers turned inward, not upward.

Julian of Norwich famously wrote, "It is in dryness and in barrenness, in sickness and in feebleness that your prayer is most pleasing . . . , even though you think it has little savor for you."[10] When the whole of our prayer life focuses on what prayer does in us or for what God does for us (or for others), we acknowledge that God's presence is not enough for us. We want more. The implications of a lifetime of never moving beyond prayer in the second degree is that we always want something from God and that we call God a good God because of the blessings God gives us.

Avoiding Prayer as Self-Therapy

A final temptation sometimes discovered in this second degree of prayer is that prayer can metamorphosize into mere mental exercises. Prayer is not

---

10. Julian of Norwich, *Revelations of Divine Love*, 14.41.

mindful meditation on a word or an ideal. Rather, prayer is direct conversation with God, either with words, mental assent, or in action. God must always be the divine subject of our prayers, for prayer is communion with God. Meditating on a word or an object is merely communing with ourselves in self-therapy. Certainly, prayers of meditation are fruit-producing endeavors in our lives—as long as the reflection is on God: Father, Son, and Holy Spirit. When I see a well-made, moving film, my mind processes the themes of the film so deeply that oftentimes my wife (in her prudence) offers to drive home. Other times, after reading a passage from a meaningful book, I find myself sitting in silence for a while, contextualizing the message of the book with my own life. In a classic sense, these examples do not describe prayer because the focus is not on Christ, but on processing themes or images from media or books. However, these meditative experiences can become prayer when we ask the Holy Spirit to reveal to us truths about God and ourselves through the objects of our meditation. If meditative prayer becomes a blessing to us, then we give thanks to God. However, if we seek a blessing, or comfort, or insight, then the focus of our prayer becomes ourselves rather than God.

Christian prayer is a combination of the subjective and the objective. It is deeply personal and intimate while also an engagement with an objective, unchanging God. Prayer involves subjective experience with God and objective doctrine of God. Sound theology is important in all areas of Christian spiritual formation to shield us from inviting into our lives various ideas and practices not found in Christianity. Tragically, the term "mindfulness," used by Buddhists to describe a nonjudgmental awareness of what one experiences in any given moment, is making its way into the field of Christian spiritual formation. Similarly, nuances of Buddhist and Hindu concepts of karma are also found in Christian spirituality today. Engaging with the insights of other religious traditions can be helpful to a degree, as long as we have a theological grounding from Scripture and the long tradition of the Christian church.

The Distinctiveness of Christian Prayer

In his last published work (which may also be his deepest theological articulation of Christian spirituality), Thomas Merton explicates the primary differences between Christianity and Zen Buddhism. While he acknowledges that both Christianity and Zen focus on objective doctrine and subjective mysticism, the primary difference he sees is that only Christianity is based on supernatural, divine revelation. Zen, conversely, seeks insight from the natural ground of being.[11] In this naturalism, adherents of Zen try to make themselves free and independent. Conversely, Christians are bound to Christ. This is why the theological aspects of prayer are vital to Christian teaching and praxis. Merton reminds us that in the first two chapters of 1 Corinthians, Paul distinguishes between two types of wisdom: One based in the world's wisdom and the other that goes beyond all human capacity to reason.[12] What makes Christian prayer unique from the prayers found in other religions is that Christian prayer transcends our ability to process or fully explain, for prayer is based in faith that we can have an intimate conversation with Almighty God, who is always speaking with us and who always desires to hear from us.

In Scripture, the word used most commonly for prayer is תְּפִלָּה, or *tephillah*, meaning an intercession or petition. When the people have a need, they make a request to God (e.g., 2 Samuel 7:27). The focus of the supplication is on God. Similarly, in the New Testament, the word προσεύχομαι, or *proseúchomai*, is commonly used, connoting an exchange of human desires with God's desires (e.g., Luke 6:12). The word for prayer in ecclesiastical Latin is consistent with Scripture: *oratio*, from which we get the word *adoratio*, or adoration of God. Christian prayer is upwardly focused, not inwardly pursued. Many times, our meditative focus on God can serendipitously lead us to personal insight. The pursuit of personal enlightenment may be helpful to us; however, if we are to pray in such a way that is consistent with the witness of Scripture, the focus of our prayers is always God. Because Christian prayer always contains an element of divine/human interaction, what we receive in prayer are not theoretical ideas that God can improve us, but actual, existential union with Christ. As Merton writes, prayer leads us to the realization that in Christ we are

> nailed to the Cross with Christ, so that the ego-self is no longer the principle of our deepest actions, which now proceed from Christ living in us. . . . It is essential to true Christianity that this experience of the Cross and self-emptying be central in the life of the Christian so that he [or she] may fully receive the Holy Spirit and know . . . all the riches of God in and through Christ.[13]

11. Merton, *Zen and the Birds of Appetite*, 45.

12. Merton, *Zen and the Birds of Appetite*, 55.

13. Merton, *Zen and the Birds of Appetite*, 55–56.

Prayer is only Christian prayer when it leads us to the cross of Christ, where we go to die to ourselves so that Christ might raise us with himself (Colossians 3:3).

The second degree of prayer stands as a primary aspect of prayer for many Christians. It's prayer modeled in Scripture, the history of the church, and is based on sound theological principles. Sadly, many Christians think that what we call the second degree of prayer, or having an intimate conversation with God, encompasses the whole of the role of prayer in our lives. Just as conversation a few times a day is not the whole relationship between two people who love each other, so we discover that Christian prayer, when properly understood, is more than speaking with God. Human capacity for prayer is far beyond conversation or thought. It involves a simplification of life, a refocusing of priorities, and a perspicuous gaze on Christ, no matter the time or circumstance. When we move beyond the second degree and into the third, we do not leave conversation with God behind! Rather, our life of prayer deepens and matures like the wood of an acoustic guitar. The older the guitar becomes, the more its tone deepens and mellows so that as it matures, it increasingly becomes a blessing to the lives of others who listen to its beautiful music.

4

The Rhythm of Prayer
(Prayer in the Third Degree)

As we waited to enter the windowless, cinder-block building downtown, my daughter and I had different thoughts running in our minds. I was concerned about the long line of people in front of us, signaling an extended stay in this drab, gray building. My sixteen-year-old daughter was concerned because she was about to take her driver's test. We made our way inside and found two rather worn metal folding chairs, where we sat waiting before her examination. Thirty-seven minutes later, an officer called her name and they left the building for our car. My nervousness for her may have surpassed her own anxiety. I desperately wanted her to do well in order to boost her confidence in driving.

As I sat in the warped chair, knee bouncing habitually, I noticed a person across the room I didn't expect to see that day. Sitting in a corner, perhaps waiting for her own child to return, was a woman in a hijab, silently praying to herself. She appeared to have no cognition of the chaos around her; instead her entire body and mind were focused on the *Salat al-zuhr*, the Muslim midday prayer. My first reaction was one of fear for her. Our community culture reflected that of the American South, in which the practitioners of religions other than Christianity are seen as suspicious. Our nation was still reeling from the attacks on September 11, 2001 and our military was still fighting in Afghanistan. Despite all of this, the faithful Muslim woman stopped to pray wherever she happened to be, even in the windowless, cinder-block driver's license exam building in the conservative American South.

My heart should have been impressed and inspired by this woman's commitment to her faith. Instead, I experienced the need to repent and ask for God's forgiveness. As a committed member of the ecumenical Lay Cistercians of Gethsemani Abbey, I (like my other LCG sisters and brothers) made a commitment before God, the abbot, the monks, and the other lay Cistercians to live according to the Cistercian charism beyond the walls of the abbey. Therefore, as part of my commitment, I follow a modified version of their liturgy of the hours, typically in the early morning, noontime, late in the afternoon, and before bed. On this day, situated in the crowded driver's license building, I opted to skip my noontime prayers. After all, I didn't want to be spiritually ostentatious. I believe the Holy Spirit allowed my life to collide with the faithful Muslim's life on that Tuesday afternoon. In that dreary, overcrowded building, I discovered that prayer was still something I had to fit into my schedule. It was not part of my life organically.

Prayer as the Rhythm of Life

When the third degree of prayer is exhibited in our lives, we don't have to think about praying. Instead, prayer becomes part of life's daily rhythms. Rhythms in the world are everywhere. The four seasons of the calendar year guide us as mile markers, serving our recollection of major and minor life events. The cyclical nature of the seasons offers stability in rapidly changing, unpredictable societies around the world. Even plants and animals rely on the stability of changing seasons in their life cycles. Removed from these seasonal rhythms, animals cannot thrive. Scientific studies have shown that human cognitive brain response is affected by the changing of the seasons, including the amount of daylight.[1] We need the natural rhythms of life for well-being and security, for they provide a sense of order in our lives, even when life does not feel particularly stable. Life patterns are important for human development as well. Young children thrive in highly systematized environments. They want to know right from wrong, the distinction between playtime and naptime, the differences between child and adult. This brings stability in a world in which they have no control and are helpless. Children without regular routines when they are young may have difficulty growing healthy habits as adults because the example set in their lives has been one of disarray rather than predictable order.

1. See *Proceedings*.

Even the most spontaneous among us have rhythms in life: we sleep at a certain time, rise at a certain time, brush our teeth regularly, clean ourselves, try to have regular meals, and partake in other daily habits. Many are blessed to gather with family at certain times of the year, celebrate birthdays, anticipate an upcoming season of our favorite sports teams, and even look forward to seasonal foods and drinks. It seems almost natural for these same types of rhythms to exist in our relationship with Christ, yet many of us keep God separate from the events in our daily planners.

Rhythms in the church year remind us of our life in Christ's life. The intersection of *chronos* (calendar time) and *kairos* (God's time) in the church year allows us to live incarnationally. Different Christian denominations refer to the seasons differently, but they all follow the same basic pattern: Advent, Christmas, Epiphany, Lent, Easter, Pentecost, and Ordinary Time. We live through these seasons as we live in Christ, following the narrative of God's engagement with the world. And the biblical lectionary is a rhythm of discipleship that allows us to read great swaths of Scripture in a rotating, three-year cycle.

When I taught preaching, I periodically had a student who believed the most engaging type of sermon was one preached extemporaneously: read the biblical text and allow the Holy Spirit to lead where he wants to lead. I admired their trust in God. I also questioned their prudence in proclaiming the gospel in a stream-of-consciousness manner. Due to the everchanging culture around us, many of us tend to live in a stream-of-consciousness way. One life event leads to the next, which leads to the next. We allow the events of life to control us, meaning we're always trying to keep up with what is happening around us. Without structure and rhythms, we can be tempted to live the same way: desiring to be led completely by mighty winds of the Holy Spirit, yet setting ourselves up to fall victim to the tempting breezes of the world. Before we know it, seasons and years pass and we wonder where the time has gone. Healthy life rhythms, particularly regarding prayer, can help us remember life's significant moments.

As a young pastor, I quickly learned that a daily planner was helpful to a degree, but one phone call could change my entire schedule that day. Life is unpredictable. We cannot always know what the next few seconds will bring. In James 4:13–15, the servant of God warns us not to be too firm in our future plans by saying that we will do this or that. James reminds his readers that life is but a mere vapor. We are not as in control of our lives as we might think we are. Instead, James exhorts us to say, "If the Lord is willing, I will . . ." This is yet another example of the cooperating aspect of prayer: we express a desire, offer it to God, and God answers through God's holy will.

Furthermore, earlier in the chapter, James addresses pride, which keeps us from drawing near to God. If we desire to control the plans of our lives, we are succumbing to pride by boasting in our intentions (v. 16). Surrendering our lives to Christ includes the surrender of all we are: our hearts, our minds, our souls, our personalities, our plans, our vocations or careers, our families—all aspects of our lives. When we can see that even our daily, weekly, and monthly calendars should be out of our control, then the inclusion of recurrent, regular conversations with God throughout our day becomes not a possibility, but an expectation.

The concept of regular, daily prayer has been a part of the history of our faith since the centuries before Christ was born. In Joshua 1:8, God instructs Joshua to meditate on God's law both day and night. In Psalm 5:3, when David prays to God in the morning, God hears him. In Psalm 55:17, David cries out to God in morning, noon, and evening. In Psalm 63:6, David writes of praying from his bed in the darkest hours of the night. Daniel prayed three times a day (Daniel 6:10). In the New Testament, we see all the people outside praying during the hour of incense burning (Luke 1:10). On several occasions, Jesus spent large amounts of time in prayer at various times throughout the day (Mark 1:35; Luke 5:16 and 6:12; John 18:1). The Apostle Peter went to a rooftop for noon prayer (Acts 10:9). In Acts 3:1, James and John went to the temple in Jerusalem for the scheduled hour of afternoon prayer. Paul refers to praying for others at all different times of the day (Colossians 1:3; 2 Thessalonians 1:11; Romans 12:12). The narrative of Scripture is consistent that times of regular prayer throughout the day are not an anomaly for some Christians, but the expectation for all of us.

Prayerful Rhythm Is Our Christian Heritage

One of the earliest accounts we have of life in the primitive, extrabiblical church comes from Hippolytus of Rome's *On the Apostolic Tradition*, dated around the year 200. In this fascinating text, we see how Christians were expected to live in society and with each other. Regarding the daily rhythm of prayer, Hippolytus writes, "The faithful, as soon as they have woken and got up, before they go to their work, shall pray to God and then hasten to their work."[2] The routine of prayer was as important to the life of early Christians as going to work. Beginning each morning with God prepares us for anything that unpredictable day might offer. For early Christians who faced potential arrest and execution, any sunrise could be their last; spending intentional time with God before they left for the day kept their eyes on God throughout the day, and in any circumstance they might have faced.

Following the example set forth in Psalm 119:164, Benedict of Nursia (b. 480), in his seminal *Rule*, established monastic communities of faith to set aside seven times each day for prayer: *vigils* (middle of the night), *lauds* (sunrise), *terce* (midmorning), *sext* (midday), *none* (midafternoon), *vespers* (sunset), and *compline* (bedtime). Every event in the monk's day becomes secondary when they hear the church bells ring, calling them to prayer. For 1,500 years, Benedictine monks have chanted the Psalms in prayer seven times a day. It normally takes them about two weeks to pray through all 150 Psalms. Imagine praying the Psalms twenty-six times a year. Over an adult lifetime, this could add up to praying the entire Psalter more than a thousand times! It's not surprising that while monks have a copy of the Psalms for reference, many chant the Psalms with their eyes closed in prayer, for the text of the Psalms have become far deeper to them than mere verses they've stored in their memories.

Millions of Christians around the world utilize resources such as *The Book of Common Prayer* to guide their times of prayer throughout the day. These texts are ripe with Scripture to guide our hearts and minds through dedicated times with God. (It's important to remember not simply to read the prayers in a prayer book, but actually to pray them.) We discover the bond that exists in the great body of Christ when millions of people pray these common prayers together. We might be separated by oceans and thousands of miles, but we are together in the throne room of heaven.

A few years ago, a student in my "Life of Prayer" class asked a question after a discussion on this monastic liturgy of the hours. "That looks like a beautiful way to spend a day," she said. "But how can we do that in the real world?" When asked a tough question, Jesus often replied by asking another one. At that moment, I decided to be like our Savior. I asked, "For the disciple of Jesus, which one is the *real world*: a day scheduled by prayer or a day led by frantic life and ministry?" Who tells us how to spend the hours and minutes of our day? Time is the universal equalizer. We each have different backgrounds, life experiences, financial means, social status,

---

2. Hippolytus, *On the Apostolic Tradition*, 35.1.

and commitments. What we all have the same is the amount of time at our disposal. Some places of employment dictate our working day down to the minute, including breaks (I've heard stories about online-shopping warehouses that do this). Some of us spend many hours a day in meetings, or teaching children in a busy classroom, or tending to patients in a hospital. We cannot fathom stopping work to pray seven times throughout the day. The issue is not what we do, but our motivations behind what we do. It's finding these prayer rhythms however they fit into our lives. Dennis Okholm reminds us that the balanced monastic life of work and prayer is no less real than our "consumptive preoccupation with gadgets, television, celebrities, war, and spirit-numbing work."[3] Have we distorted reality or have monastic communities?

One easy way to begin is to adjust the free time we have in a day. It could be during a commute to work and back, how we spend a lunch break, what media (if any) we invite into our lives in the evenings. It could mean waking up twenty minutes earlier than usual or changing our end-of-day routines. Prayer in the third degree does not always require a monumental life shift. Sometimes all it takes is a small change of course in our trajectory. Pilots have an axiom called the "one in sixty rule." By changing a flight trajectory by just one degree, a course changes by one mile for every sixty miles flown. Sometimes all our lives require is a small shift in priorities, in our focus or our scope. During my many years in pastoral ministry, I began a system of scheduling several meetings a day in my calendar. When I was blessed to have a church secretary on staff, he or she would know when I was available and when I was in one of these meetings. Of course, the meetings were with God, scattered throughout the day, in which I would follow my own divine office, tailored to my schedule. On the days I would be with a family in a hospital during one of these scheduled meetings, I made it a practice to stop in the hospital chapel on my way out, or to sit in my car in the parking lot for my fifteen- to twenty-minute prayer time. Since not all days look the same, flexibility is necessary. We must not forget to be gracious to ourselves, for surely God is gracious toward us. The important issue to remember is that the act of praying is not as important as our motivation in praying. In Jeremiah 6, the Lord speaks through the prophet that because the people's hearts were not right with God and their motivations impure, God was tired of their many sacrificial offerings and

---

3. Okholm, *Monk Habits for Everyday People*, 32.

prayers. If we craft prayer time throughout our day simply to do something spiritual in a materialistic life, perhaps it would be best not to pray.

Prayer as Community

Another way to create healthy rhythms of prayer in our lives is through a shared commitment with others. Monastic communities thrive because everyone is committed to the same ideals and has taken the same vows. When we surround ourselves with others who share our prayerful approach to life, we find the rhythms of life (including our prayer life) are expectations not just of ourselves but of the entire community. Examples from chapters 2 and 4 of the book of Acts show the close connections they had with each other. However, it's difficult to be on our own and maintain holy motivations for living. We may need to step away from certain groups or friends who don't share our approach to life. As Bernard wrote to Pope Eugenius, "The guilty are not shamed by the consciences of others who are guilty; where all are filthy, the stench of one is hardly noticed."[4] We need holy people around us to offer loving corrections when they see our spiritual fruit has become inedible. Of course, the converse is true as we speak into the lives of others. We can't offer life adjustments to them based on what we can't see in their hearts, but only through their words and actions. When the motivation of speaking into each other's lives is holy love and not criticism or condemnation, the Holy Spirit can strengthen ties between people in addition to any personal bolstering one might receive.

Authenticity in Prayerful Rhythms

As late as the fifth century, the early Christians intentionally kept the unconverted from even hearing the words of the Lord's Prayer. The idea was that if a pre-Christian person prayed the words without understanding the deep spiritual mystery and power behind them, they might do damage to their souls by praying to the "Father, who art in heaven," without yet having been spiritually adopted by God the Father through Christ.[5] Perhaps this is similar to the Apostle Paul's exhortation in 1 Corinthians 11:27 not to receive the Lord's Supper *unworthily*. This adverb reminds us to approach

4. Bernard, *Five Books on Consideration*, I.13.
5. Ambrose, *Of the Sacraments*, 5.18.

the holy actions of our lives with the right focus, personal motivations, and with a holy perspective that respects what it is we are about to do. When we schedule prayer for the sake of having it in our schedule, we should be careful to follow through with the holy intention of desiring to be with God for unobstructed, focused time with the great love of our lives.

You may remember the parable of Jesus about the father and his two sons, found in Matthew 21:28–32. The father says to one of his sons, "I need you to work in the vineyard." The son replied, "No way!" Later, he changed his mind and set to work. The father went to the other son and said the same thing. "Sure, I'll go," was the son's reply; but he never went. Jesus then asks the pertinent question: "Which of the two sons did what his father wanted?" Of course, the answer is the first son, because he actually did what his father asked. Putting times of prayer on our calendar doesn't mean we're engaging in prayer. Perhaps we're seeking the appearance of being holy but without the responsibility therein. Saying we are going to pray is not actually praying. Perhaps you have known someone struggling with a life crisis, and after having a conversation with them, you say, "I'll be praying for you." Will you pray for them, or like the second son in the parable will you say something to please them and then forget to pray? Perhaps this spiritually comforting statement to a struggling friend was nothing more than a way to end your conversation. Rather than telling a friend you will be praying for her, perhaps you stop and pray right then, no matter where you are. When we're living in the third degree of prayer, our first instinct is to pray. We are always ready to pray, and like Paul's exhortation to Timothy regarding preaching, we are prepared in season and out of season to have an intimate conversation with Almighty God.

Before texting became commonplace, my wife and I had to wait until evening to catch up on the events of each other's day. I remember she had much more to say in describing her daily events than I did! Now we can send each other text messages from a meeting or while walking to get a cup of coffee. We know what each other is doing all the time. To me, it's as if I'm with her, despite being in separate places. When I first taught at a seminary in Europe a few years ago, it was the first time in a decade that we weren't able to communicate with each other instantly. Since I couldn't afford to have cell service in the Netherlands, I couldn't walk through historic neighborhoods with an eye on my phone, describing to her what I was seeing. I'd have to wait until I had wireless Internet service so we could have a video chat, usually once a day. We felt isolated from each other because we weren't immediately available for one another. Prayer in the third degree is the blessed awareness of knowing that we can converse with God throughout our day, not just at specific, scheduled times.

The Instinctiveness of Prayer

In this degree of prayer, conversation with God becomes our first response when receiving big news of any kind. Many years ago I knew a woman who daily watched the evening news from her video recorder so she could pause the broadcast after every news story and pray for the people involved. She understood that the Holy Spirit could transform a secular newscast into a sacred event. Our son had this awareness, as well, even when he was a toddler. When a siren-blaring ambulance would speed past us, he would shout, "An ambulance! We need to pray for that person!" One of us would then pray for the unknown patient in the back of the ambulance and the person driving. Most of us don't have the spiritual sensitivity our young son had and we must allow the Holy Spirit to grow it in us. Like plants, this awareness grows quickly in some of us, but in others, it takes more time. Spiritual growth is incomparable, for God has created us unique from every other person in history. Trying to compare our growth in Christ with someone else's is prideful folly that can lead to frustration and anxiety.

When I was in seminary, two very different professors spoke life into me for three years. One of them, Old Testament scholar John Oswalt, invited me to meet with him and a few other students each Friday at noon for prayerful accountability. It was a good time—sometimes a difficult and convicting time—when Dr. Oswalt prayed for the Holy Spirit to convict you of sin and fill you with spiritual fruit. The other faculty member, Jerry Mercer, was my preaching and spiritual formation professor. Jerry had a way of seeing the great things of God in the minutiae, and his joy for life was magnetic. One day when I arrived at his office, I opened the door and was hit by a thick reddish, fragrant smoke. "Come in," he said, "I'm sitting in the presence of the Lord allowing my prayers to rise to God like incense!" A visit to Mercer's office was an entirely different experience than visiting Oswalt's, yet they each demonstrated a deep love for Jesus and the essence of a holy life.

Motivations in Prayer

Knowing what motivates us is key to discerning the nature of our relationship with Christ. Scheduling prayer throughout the week or attending daily prayer meetings are wonderful, as long as our motivation for these events leads to humble submission before God and not a feeling of personal pride because we've included these in our day. Sometimes, the closer we grow in a life of prayer, the more we realize just how far from God we really are. In *The Imitation of Christ*, Thomas à Kempis writes, "We must examine both our inner thoughts and our external actions and put them in order, for both have an important part to play in our spiritual advancement."[6] Daily examination of our love for God can help keep the rhythms of prayer normalized in our lives. The Ignatian *Examen* has been helpful for some people in this regard. The steps of this discipline are varied, but they involve a nightly reflection on our events of the day: What we did, what we thought, the role of God in our day, etc. The thought of prayer as a rhythm of life makes for a good book topic, but in the real world of life in the twenty-first century, it's easy to begin well but soon find ourselves ready to move on to the next new spiritual trend. Perhaps this is why motivation remains a key component of the third degree of prayer.

Obstacles to Perseverance

I've discovered at least three reasons why people find it difficult to persevere in the third degree of prayer. The first is our distracted, multitasked lives. I'm intentionally going to avoid the ongoing debate of whether or not modern humans have a shorter attention span than goldfish. (No offense to goldfish, but I refuse to believe that.) What we do know is that in a time in which multitasking is seen as a productivity necessity in both work and life, recent research published by MIT Press sees multitasking in a different way. In *The Distracted Mind*, research scientists Adam Gazzaley and Larry D. Rosen reveal that our brains were not designed for constant switching of foci. Our brains do not multitask, but rather switch rapidly between tasks. These rapid transitions bring an unsteadiness to our brains, which were designed to focus on one task at a time. This brings anxiety, rather than

---

6. à Kempis, *Imitation of Christ*, I.19.3.

contentment, to our lives. According to this research, the rise of personal media devices has brought these brain distractions to a heightened level.[7]

If you've ever had a conversation with someone and their smartphone beeps with a new text message, one of two things is invariably going to happen: 1) They look at you apologetically and check their phone; 2) They continue listening to you but their half-hidden facial expression tells you they're wanting to check their phone. The truth is that we find it difficult to remain focused on one person or a single task because we invite distractions into our lives. Perhaps we feel that the more productive we are, the more valuable we are as a person or as an employee. The attempt to multitask not only inhibits production, it reduces the quality of the work we produce and diminishes the view others have of their worth to us.

Distractions in our relationship with God are no different. Our spiritual attention spans are directly related to the number of focus-destroying devices and priorities we invite into our lives. I once observed a college student watching a football game on TV, texting a friend on his phone, and reading a textbook that was on his lap. I have doubts as to his productiveness in any of those endeavors. How can we maintain a daily rhythm of prayer with so many objects that take our focus off of God? The follower of Christ is called to have a singular focus. In Luke 10:42, Jesus teaches Martha that she is worried and upset about so many things that are distracting her. Instead, she should focus on only necessary thing, as Mary has done. Each of us who are followers of Christ should make seeking God the *unum necessarium*, or one necessary thing of our lives. When we become distracted, we become like Martha, forgetting what is really important in life. The writer of Hebrews reminds us in 12:2 to keep our eyes on Jesus, who is the author and the perfecter of our faith. Our eyes belong to God, as do our motivations, our actions, our priorities, and every other aspect of our lives. If something exists in our lives that takes our eyes off of Jesus, we should ask ourselves why that something is in our lives in the first place. Of course, having exterior simplicity in our lives must first come from an interior simplicity, in which our heart is set on God alone.[8]

Simplifying our lives involves more than merely cleaning out our closets or living in a tiny house, for even empty closets and small homes cannot rid our minds of distractions. In his important work *A Plain Account of Christian Perfection*, John Wesley, knowing that his life with God was not

---

7. Elhai et al., "The Relationship."

8. General Chapter, *The Spirit of Simplicity*, 67.

yet where it needed to be, refers to Book II, Chapter 4 of *The Imitation of Christ*, which refers to having simplicity of intention and purity of affection.[9] Both of these holy men know that without simplicity in our life's purpose and holy purity in our hearts, we have not given all of who we are to Christ, for we are still distracted by what we assume to be important concerns in the world. When we refuse to allow the Holy Spirit to remove the clutter from our lives, the clutter becomes our life's center rather than God.

Simplifying our life involves simplifying the motivations and desires of our lives. If Christ is everything to us, why would we want to shift our focus to anything else? Brother Lawrence of the Resurrection wrote about his distractions in prayer. He desperately tried to be a good monk, but he thought about other things during community prayer and he'd fall asleep during mass. For more than a decade, he felt as if he was a walking disappointment to God. He grew to realize that prayer could take place anywhere and not just in the sanctuary. As he repaired shoes, he'd pray for the person who would wear them. When he was preparing meals or washing the dishes, he would give thanks to God for his sustaining grace. Turning our distractions into prayer can be helpful to us when our minds are occupied by so very many things. If we do not simplify our lives, which lead to a smaller number of distractions, we can succumb to the next great obstacle to living in the third degree of prayer.

Temptation becomes an obstacle for us when we forget that we belong to God. When what we love and desire is outside of God's love and intention for us, we attempt to soothe our heart's unsettledness with artificial balm. Merely hiding our heart's clutter in a closet is not eliminating it from our lives, for we can still rummage through it to seek artificial solace. The continued presence of this clutter, even though it remains hidden in our heart's storeroom, remains a constant temptation to us, for when a situation arises in which we need God, our first inclination is to forage through the closet for that which we believe will come to our aid. Temptation in prayer seeps to the surface when we falsely believe that we're able in our own strength to maintain this life of prayer in the third degree. The Holy Spirit is the motivator, the empowerer, and the love that gives us the capacity always to be ready to pray, no matter where we are or in what situation we may find ourselves.

When our lives are filled with distractions, we often find ourselves facing temptations. These temptations can then lead us to frustration, which is

9. Wesley, *A Plain Account of Christian Perfection*, 366–67.

the opposite of contentment in Christ. The focus of our frustration can be ourselves or it can be God. We become frustrated with ourselves when we realize that we know better than to allow distractions and temptations to rule our lives. Our tendency is then to abandon this third degree of prayer, as we simply don't have the resolve to maintain it. Until we acknowledge that we are helpless and in no way have the capacity to maintain anything in our strength, this frustration will only become heightened. Perhaps we become frustrated with ourselves because, in the words of Teresa of Avila, we know there are rooms in the castle of our lives where we do not fellowship intimately with God.[10] When we experience these self-frustrations, it's helpful to ask the Holy Spirit to reveal to us the places in our lives we have not completely submitted to God. The benefit of self-frustration is that we have a realization that all is not well with our souls, which sometimes manifests itself as shame. Many times the mere acknowledgment of an issue is all we need for the Holy Spirit to minister to us, replacing the frustration and shame with God's peace and grace. As one monk at Gethsemani Abbey shared with me, "Mistakes can be our teachers rather than our undertakers." It's all a matter of perspective.

Frustration with God is another matter. When we become frustrated with God, the issue is that God has not done what we wanted God to do, or God has not moved in our designated time frame, or in what we deem is the proper way. This can happen when we use prayer for our own selfish means. Our growth in Christ is not exclusively for ourselves. The Holy Spirit moves in our lives so we might be a blessing to others. In our scheduled, set-apart times of prayer, our souls become ovens where spiritual bread is baked to feed those around us.

Prayerful Rhythm as Trust in God

In Isaiah 36–37 (see also 2 Kings 19 and 2 Chronicles 32), we have an account of a dilemma facing King Hezekiah. He had received word that the powerful Assyrians were coming to visit, ensuring utter doom for the kingdom. Hezekiah knew that as King Sennacherib of Assyria had done with other nations, he would send an emissary to Jerusalem with a message that to avoid destruction and mass murder, they were to hand over their storehouses of gold. The nation would become part of Assyria, but at least the people would be allowed to live.

10. Teresa of Avila, *Interior Castle*, I.4.

When the emissary from Assyria delivered the terrifying and devastating news to the people of Jerusalem and Hezekiah, the king tore his robes in grief. His counselors began to strategize and calculate what the best response would be. Should they ask Egypt to come to their aid? Should they begin stockpiling the nation's gold? They waited for Hezekiah to call them together and create a strategic plan. The king sent his most trusted leaders to the prophet Isaiah to receive God's instructions. Isaiah's counsel was simply to pray and trust God. Trusting God rather than those in his own court, Hezekiah went into the temple to pray that the Lord would protect them. Just as the offended and angry Assyrian army was about to obliterate little Jerusalem, the army mysteriously left and returned in embarrassment to Nineveh, the Assyrian capital. When the third degree of prayer is a reality in our lives, our first response when facing a crisis is to pray, to seek help from the power of God rather than in a human strategic plan.

In the late 1940s, Asbury Theological Seminary began construction on a chapel building. Digging through the Kentucky limestone was expensive and time-consuming, but the community pulled together to see the foundation dug. Due to financial shortcomings and a lack of lumber during World War II, construction on the chapel was halted. Asbury's president at the time, J. C. McPheeters, faced a dire situation. He could have sent a bulletin to seminary donors or fashioned a strategic plan. Instead, like Hezekiah thousands of years before, his first inclination was to pray. While the recollections of what happened next are varied, the bottom line is that a lumber truck, stacked with the lumber the chapel needed, broke down on the road in front of the seminary. The driver took pennies on the dollar for his load and the chapel construction continued. Since the seminary is located on a road that dead-ends at the Kentucky River, the presence of a large truck in town made the miracle even more astonishing.

Both King Hezekiah and J. C. McPheeters could have made decisions based on human counsel and planning. They may have been seen as competent leaders for doing so. However, the internal, Holy Spirit discernment each of them had told them to trust God. I have discovered that many pastors and local churches have forgotten this principle. Without a doubt, the Holy Spirit can work through leadership development, the structuring of strategic plans, and the formulation of financial giving algorithms. However, when these approaches are our first response to a crisis, we demonstrate to others that our trust is in ourselves rather than in God. Like Hezekiah and J. C. McPheeters, we simply must trust God and not be tempted to trust our capacity to handle situations.

Seeing God in All of It

It's a mistake to think that we "make progress" in the spiritual life like we might with a diet or exercise plan. Prayer might deepen our love for God, but that shouldn't be our goal. Just because we cannot sometimes see God working in our lives does not mean that God is not working in our lives. God remains ever present in us, even though God sometimes chooses to remain in the background. The seemingly absent presence of God in the book of Esther is a familiar example of this. Often, we look for the explicit presence of God when perhaps we should be looking for the implicit presence of God. God works in our lives through multiple methods, many of which we cannot discern at the time. Bernard of Clairvaux offered three ways God ministers to us when we may not be able to perceive it. First, God lifts our minds from worldly attachments so we might cling to him. Second, God confers on us divine knowledge so we might have insight into heavenly wisdom. Finally, God fosters our love of heavenly goodness, so that, while still living in human flesh, we might rise above the flesh to seek God's divine love.[11]

Prayer in the third degree compels us to see God in all things, and in all things we allow intimate conversation with God to be what guides us, even when we cannot perceive God working. When we acknowledge that God is indeed working in and through our lives, our frustrations fade away because our prayers are becoming less inner introspection and more response to God's loving grace. Living in response to God, rather than in expectation of God, is the surest way to live in that peace that surpasses all understanding (Philippians 4:7). This describes the daily rhythm of prayer.

11. Bernard, *The Parables & The Sentences*, 139.

5

Living Prayer (Prayer in the Fourth Degree)

THE AIR WAS COOL and crisp as I made my way through the woods on the familiar path to the statues. The trail led me past the lake, up the steps, and when I made it to the prayer shelter, I entered to read over some of the prayer requests. People dealing with a myriad of struggles and anxieties leave them here—prayers for physical or spiritual healing, prayers of confession, prayers for a recovery of hope, and others. I'm not sure if Jeremiah literally consumed God's Word (Jeremiah 15:16), but the mice sure eat the dozens of prayer requests left in the little shelter. On that day I remember thinking how St. Francis of Assisi would have approved of the rodents' papered feast. I paused and prayed over several requests, and left the rest to God, knowing that God's providential grace was already with those who were seeking prayers from the faithful.

On this day in late October, most of the colorful leaves were already on the ground, except for a few stragglers that were gently descending to the forest floor below. A friend once told me that she prefers to see trees without their leaves, because then we can see the trees for who they really are, not hidden behind their leaves. I was on my way to "the Statues," as they're commonly called at Gethsemani Abbey. They're compelling works of art in the middle of the wild lands across the road from the monastery. The wooded trail makes a right turn and you're suddenly upon them: the disciples of Jesus fast asleep in the garden of Gethsemane. I have made this hike on many occasions, yet the Holy Spirit asks me the same question each time I see them: "Are you asleep in your faith?" The path continues beyond the sleeping disciples and up a small hill. As you ascend, your eyes cannot miss the statue before you. Jesus, kneeling high on his knees with his hands covering his face in agony and terror, is pouring out his heart to his Father. Words cannot describe the beautifully horrific wonder of this work of art in the woods.

On this day, as I sat on a tree stump prayerfully meditating upon the statue before me, I noticed something strange about the face of Jesus. Because the statue is sized larger than life and Jesus' face is near the top and covered by his hands, most of his face is hidden. I stepped closer to the statue and stood on its base to get a better look. On Jesus' mouth, held in place by the deserted remnants of a spider web, was a small, single yellow leaf. I got back down and could not take my mind off of it. Of all the places this little leaf could have fallen, it landed on the sacred lips of Jesus. In my wonder I imagined this leaf choosing to land there despite the cries of its fellow leaves to join them on the decaying ground below. In that moment, tears streaming down my cold cheeks, I confessed I wasn't sure where I would land. Has my life landed on the lips of my Savior or have I merely been following everyone to the decomposing world below?

The Little Leaf

The fourth degree of prayer is exemplified by that little yellow leaf. It's a life that exists close to the mouth of God. Prayer in the fourth degree is living with Jesus in the garden of Gethsemane. At that moment in Jesus' life, the Savior was positioned between life and death, or heaven and earth. Jesus in the garden exemplified the incarnate one: completely God and completely human. When we become the little leaf on the lips of Jesus, we become intimately one with Christ in his humanity and in his divinity. Jesus doesn't merely invite us to hear words from his sacred lips. Instead, our Lord invites us to take residence on those lips. As we take residence on the praying lips of Jesus, the desire of our lives is to be with Christ, and in Christ, even as he prays in agony in the garden and faces the cross. Our prayer is that the cross we're called to bear might become joyful surrender rather than a lifelong burden and sacrifice.

Since the era of the church fathers, Christians have written extensively about images of spiritual intimacy such as this one. In fact, the entire Song of Songs in Scripture has been seen as an allegory of Christ's love for humanity. For example, church father Theodoret of Cyrus (d. 457) sees the kiss described in Song of Songs 1:2 as "not the joining of mouths, but the communion of the holy soul and the divine Word."[1] Ambrose of Milan (d. 397) nuances this a bit differently: "When God the Word kisses us, he enlightens our heart and governing faculty with the spirt of the knowledge of God."[2] This approach to mystical theology may make some of us uncomfortable, but when we ponder its deeper meanings, it's really true that God's love for us is more intimate than any love shared between husband and wife. In his second of eighty-six sermons on the Song of Songs, Bernard of Clairvaux describes this kiss with a paraphrase of 1 Timothy 2:5: "The kiss . . . that takes its being both from the giver and the receiver, is a person that is formed by both, none other than 'the one mediator between God and mankind, himself a man, Christ Jesus.'"[3] Jesus himself, described in the theology of the two natures, is the kiss of God to humanity.

When we're living in the fourth degree of prayer, intimate conversation with God is natural because Christ has become our life (Colossians 3:4). We have no idea that we're praying because we're just living as one empowered by God's Spirit. Because our entire existence is in Christ, we begin to see the world and the people of the world as God does. What the world offers has no meaning for us, for like that little leaf, we are content to exist on the lips of Christ. As Paul exhorts in 1 Thessalonians 5:17, we are to "pray without ceasing" or "unceasingly." The adverb "unceasingly" used in this verse connotes that which has no spaces in between intervals of time. Prayer in our lives should be as consistent as the seconds ticking away on a clock, or as constant as the flow of water in a river. Our life becomes one perpetual prayer to God. This can only happen when we become a leaf on the lips of Jesus. In his final thoughts on prayer before his untimely death, Thomas Merton shares that "prayer is not just part of our life . . . but an expression of who we are; our very being expresses itself with prayer because prayer flows from our relation to God and to other people . . ."[4] Without a life of prayer, we have no life in Christ, Merton writes, for this prayerful life is evidence of God dwelling within us.

In his moving testimonial text *He Leadeth Me*, Walter Ciszek writes that "real prayer occurs . . . when at last we find ourselves in the presence of God. Then every thought becomes the father to a prayer, and words quite

1. Theodoret, *Commentary on the Song of Songs*, I.

2. Ambrose, *On Isaac and the Soul*, 3.8–9.

3. Bernard, *Sermons on the Song of Songs*, 10.

4. Merton, "On Prayer."

often are superfluous."[5] Prayer in the fourth degree is prayer that doesn't have to be prayed. It's a loving relationship with God similar to the love between two people who have been married for fifty years. Because they know each other so well, words become meaningless in their communication. In the fourth degree of prayer, conversation with God becomes as natural to us as our next breath, because without it our souls wouldn't be able to survive. Prayer becomes our life in Christ, and our life in Christ becomes our prayer. We have an awareness of God's love to us, in us, and through us. A life without God seems unimaginable to us, and a moment without God seems unbearable. In sharing the testimony of a woman she admired, Methodist writer and teacher Phoebe Palmer (d. 1874) writes that this woman did not approach a holy life linearly. Instead, this woman's deep love for God was "not only a heart holiness, but a holy walk, a holy life, a holy conversation, a life of entire symmetrical holiness."[6] Palmer longed for this same type of all-encompassing love for God for herself, in which the Holy Spirit would transform all aspects of her life into a living prayer.

Abiding in the Vine

We cannot strive to maintain this kind of life, for we're without the capacity to cling to an almighty, holy God. Instead, Jesus tells us to abide in him (John 15:4). Abiding in Christ is becoming infused into Christ the vine. We don't become the vine; we are the branches receiving spiritual nourishment from the vine. For many of us used to doing great things for God, the idea of abiding seems counterproductive! However, in that same verse in John's Gospel, Jesus says that unless we abide in him, we cannot produce fruit. In his commentary on John 15, John Wesley wrote that abiding in Christ involves a deeper connection to Christ than merely communing with others in the body of Christ.[7] True abiding in Christ is deep spiritual communion with Christ himself. This produces holiness in our hearts and life, of which prayer and faithful living are spiritual fruit. Any concept or definition of discipleship that does not begin and end with the idea of abiding in Christ is useless, for the energy and motivation for disciple-making ministries will be of human, rather than divine, effort.

---

5. Ciszek and Flaherty, *He Leadeth Me*, 61.

6. Palmer, *The Promise of the Father*, 368.

7. Wesley, *Explanatory Notes Upon the New Testament*, John XV.6.

Behind the statue of the sleeping disciples in the Gethsemani Abbey woods is a network of thriving vines. Several shoots emerging from the main vines anchored on the ground below have found their way up the tree trunks. Several of these vines hang from a tree limb that's just above the statue of the sleeping disciples. Ironically, the effigy of the slumbering followers of Jesus is not connected anywhere to this network of flourishing foliage. Instead, surrounding this statue is rocky dirt, dried twigs, and dead leaves. Like the disciples depicted in this meaningful statue, our faith slumbers and we separate ourselves from Christ when we are not abiding in the one true vine. The vine of Christ is all around us. We admire its beauty. We are in awe at its life. However, just because we can see the vine with our eyes doesn't mean we're abiding in that vine. Similarly, sometimes we are unable to see that which is closest to us. When I lose my reading glasses, I search all over the house until I scratch my head in frustration and discover my glasses have been there the entire time. We have all experienced difficult life situations in which we search to find God. We look for some concrete evidence of God's presence that can reassure us that we're not alone. This is looking for God with a willing, weak flesh, rather than in the peace of our souls. We cannot keep watch and pray (Matthew 26:41) when, unlike that little leaf on the lips of Jesus, the focus of our lives is on how tired we are rather than on how resilient the Holy Spirit is in our lives. When we live in the fourth degree of prayer, we have the assurance of knowing that we have found sanctuary in the grace of God by abiding in the life-giving vine of Christ.

Theosis

So far in this chapter we've alluded to it, but perhaps before we go any further a mention should be made about *theosis*. In some Christian traditions, the idea of becoming "one with God" is a major aspiration. Because we join with God in theosis, humanity regains the capacity to return to a human state as we were before the fall by Adam and Eve. We might become holy as God himself is holy. This seems like a daring, spiritually prideful thought! If we have the capacity to be like God, does that make us God?

A primary patristic authority for the concept of theosis is the revered church father Athanasius of Alexandria (d. 373), whose unchanging theological steadfastness on the nature of the incarnate Son of God is accepted as orthodox teaching to this day. Adherents to the possibility of theosis cite

Athanasius's famous line, "He was made man that we might be made God."[8] However, in the very next sentence, Athanasius explains this statement: "and He manifested Himself by a body that we might receive the idea of the unseen Father; and He endured the insolence of men that we might inherit immortality." Athanasius carefully articulates that Christ's incarnation has a lasting effect on us. Because Christ lowered himself to become one of us, and because we are salvifically attached to Christ, we are exalted by Christ in an incarnational way. Thomas Aquinas explains that Christ's incarnation allows humanity to share in the full participation of the Trinitarian Godhead, which is "the true bliss of [humanity] and end of human life."[9] However, while we share in Christ's incarnation, we will never ontologically be like Christ, for we are created beings and not of the same substance with God the Father, as Jesus is. In his description of the fourth degree of love for God, St. Bernard writes that just as a drop of water appears to disappear in a glass of wine, so do people who love God this deeply seem to disappear in God. Bernard is careful to explain that the elements of the drop of water still exist in the wine, even though we cannot see them; the water doesn't lose its substance. Likewise, we do not lose our identity when we love God in the deepest way humanly possible on earth, even though we seem to disappear to ourselves in God. As Paul writes in Colossians 3:3, "For you died, and your life is hidden with Christ in God." Being hidden with Christ is to set our minds on what matters above and not on earthly matters. Christ hides us from the snares of this world when we die to the world.

The concept of theosis is an intriguing one, and helpful in describing what we call prayer in the fourth degree. However, as beings created in the image and likeness of God, our identity has divine value and worth. To be swallowed up in God to the extent that we no longer exist would deny the intrinsic value of our creation, and an individual's eternal soul would be eradicated, which would have eschatological implications, as well.

A Missiological Perspective

Prayer in the fourth degree is becoming prayer to such an extent that people see God in us before they see us. If we shine a flashlight towards someone in a dark room, that person doesn't see us behind the light, for the light's radiance consumes that person's vision. As we mirror the blazing glory of God

8. Athanasius, *On the Incarnation*, 54.3.

9. Aquinas, *Summa Theologica* 3.1.2.

into the world around us we become the light of the world (Matthew 5:14). John Wesley wrote that when the holiness of our lives shines in this way, we cannot hide the light inside of us anymore than we can hide the sun from the sky.[10] Our importance means nothing to us, so long as others are able to be illuminated by the light of God emanating from our lives. However, when we attempt to light the world with a light other than Christ, the light soon goes out and we can actually do harm to others. As Bernard of Clairvaux wrote, "A light that has gone out not only puts everything into darkness, but it also spreads a terrible odor."[11] One guide that we are indeed living in this fourth degree of prayer is the awareness that the light of Christ we shine is the light of our own lives and not the light of someone else. "Those who do not shine with their own light," Bernard continues, "shine as hypocrites with a borrowed light, as they are not on fire themselves."[12]

In this approach to prayer and life, temptation has no control over us. In fact, because both our hearts and our activities are continually contemplating Christ in us, the temptations of the world are no longer obstacles. Rather than merely something we try to avoid, sin becomes the exception in our lives. This happens when, by the grace of the Holy Spirit, we are able to see the world through the eyes of God. We see Christ in all circumstances, in all people, and in every interaction we have with others. Let's be clear: tragedies happen that shake us deeply for many years and change the trajectories of our lives. Life in the fourth degree of prayer is the grace to have an eternal perspective on the hurts and wounds we obtain in the battles of life. An eternal perspective of life puts illness and even death in perspective. For the believer in Christ, death is not the end of life, but a mere transition to a new life in the eternal church.

No Doubt

Several years ago, I visited a parishioner who had admitted herself to a mental hospital. This occasion was not the first time she had done this, for she had struggled for years to overcome chronic, crippling depression and daily thoughts of suicide. After I passed the various security gates and documentary protocols at the hospital, I entered her windowless room, sparsely appointed with only a bed and a single metal chair, both bolted

10. Wesley, *Explanatory Notes on the New Testament*, Matt V.14.

11. Bernard, *Letters*, 173.

12. Bernard, *Letters*, 173.

to the floor. I sat down and attempted to engage her with a smile and reassuring greeting. Despite her weary and heavily medicated countenance, we had a wonderful conversation that afternoon, highlighted by a pivotal comment she made about halfway through my visit. "Mike," she said, "I have an overwhelming sense of a heavy darkness over me. I can't stop thinking of ways to kill myself. Yet more than ever before in my life, I've never felt Jesus closer to me than he is right now." By the grace of God, this sister in Christ had the spiritual capacity to differentiate mental illness from her relationship with God. Suicidal depression did not define her. She was a little leaf on the lips of Jesus who happened to be dealing with an enduring mental disorder. Her many years of mental suffering contributed to a relationship with Christ that most of us will never be able to appreciate. She personified the thoughts of Thomas à Kempis when he wrote, "All our peace in the wretched world comes from our humble endurance of suffering and not from living a life without it."[13]

For some, human suffering may actually become a means to that intimate peace with Christ. Jesus doesn't come to our aid when we're in need of divine help. In fact, Jesus doesn't come to our aid at all because he never leaves us in the first place. Asking God to be with us during difficult times is no different than asking our heart to start beating before exercise. When we live in this fourth degree of prayer, we never doubt God's presence in us, with us, and through us, because we have a constant awareness of God no matter what situation we face.

The Danger of Noise

Living in this fourth degree of prayer seems like a virtuous ideal if one is living in a monastery or off the grid in a forest. For those of us who live a hectic, twenty-first-century lifestyle, however, this might seem an idealistic impossibility. It is difficult enough for us to remember where we placed our car keys, let alone be in constant, prayerful awareness of God's presence in our lives. The thought of life becoming a living prayer when dealing with difficult co-workers, clients, or that unfocused driver who almost veered into our car on the expressway may seem unimaginable. Certainly, living in society has its distractions, but if we are not able to remove ourselves from society, then we must transition our approach to life in society.

---

13. à Kempis, *Imitation of Christ*, II.3.3.

What I have discovered in myself is that the obstacles to a life in the fourth degree of prayer are not in the society or community around me, but inside me. For example, I complain of the noise of the world that interrupts my focus on God until I'm in a completely quiet room and I'm still hearing the noise. Much of the noise in our lives isn't exterior, or from the outside world. Instead, it's interior, from our own inner worlds. We might retreat to a quiet place of refuge from the pandemonium of life, but the world's noise and chaos is still with us. This noise could be unrepentant sin, an unhealed past, or simply our sense that we're too in love with all the world has to offer. One helpful exercise is to set a timer for five minutes and sit quietly. At the end of the five minutes, write down all of the thoughts that went through your mind. Be honest and write everything down. It could be items not to forget at the grocery store, work deadlines, lustful thoughts, or even wondering how much time is left until the timer buzzes. Why did these specific items disrupt your time of stillness, and what is it about these items that is indicative about the role these distractions have in your life?

The noise around us might always be present, but the noise inside of us doesn't need to be there. Sanctifying our distractions might be helpful to us. In his book *Into the Silent Land*, Martin Laird offers some helpful guidance in this regard.[14] Trying to push away our distractions, he states, only causes our frustrations to escalate, which creates new distractions. Whereas Laird encourages us to remember a prayer word to help us deal with distractions, I find it more helpful to pray the distraction: "Lord, I'm worried about the many bills we have to pay each month. Help me place them in perspective that financial security is nothing compared to placing my trust in you." The reality is that we willingly invite the noise of the world into our lives no matter where we are. When the great Christian writers of the past referred to avoiding the many distractions of life, many times they were writing to monastics! One example is Thomas à Kempis: "Do not cling to short-lived things, otherwise, you will get caught in their webs and perish."[15] Certainly the lives of the monks who read these words had much more simplicity than our complex daily mazes. Our crazy schedules may not go away, but we control the importance these activities have in our lives.

14. Laird, *Into the Silent Land*, 79.

15. à Kempis, *Imitation of Christ*, II.1.4.

Being Led by the Spirit and Not by the World

When our daughter was young, I remember driving her to an event with our local church. As I drove down a highway, a driver pulled out of a side road right in front of us. I slammed the brake pedal and expressed my frustration verbally—and loudly. From her backseat booster chair, our daughter said calmly and with great concern, "Daddy, maybe that driver is just having a bad day and didn't pay attention." My first reaction was annoyance. Hers was concern for the other driver. The result of the event was our prayer for that driver as I stared at his taillights for several miles down the highway. Jesus, the incarnate Son of God, sent by God the Father to be the propitiation of our sins, has left the Holy Spirit to dwell in our lives. Why, then, do we allow the small frustrations of life to devour us? This is the opposite of the fourth degree of prayer, for we willingly invite the noise of the world to dwell in our minds, hearts, and even souls. Of all people, we disciples should know better than this, yet these reactions to the world's noise persists in many of our lives.

One reason I believe this happens is related to a second obstacle to life in the fourth degree of prayer: our love for the world. God is love, and we are charged to love others as God loves them. However, this does not mean loving all the world has to offer. Sometimes a restlessness in our lives is the reason we long for the newest fashions, the most updated electronic devices, or that dream vacation. Contentment with that which God has already blessed our lives is a wonderful grace. Again, Thomas à Kempis instructs us that "there is no peace in the heart of one who is . . . attached to worldly things. Peace is found only in one who is fervent and spiritual."[16] What worldly things in a monastery could be creating disorder in the hearts of the monks reading these words? They are the ones who have left the temptations of the world beyond their monastic walls. However, loving the world is loving more than the "stuff" of the world. We love the world when we concern ourselves with our reputation in the eyes of others. We love the world when we focus on obtaining as much knowledge as possible. We love the world when we strive to be as holy and complete as we can be. It all becomes noise that keeps up from hearing the whispers of God's voice in the innermost places of our lives.

A love for the world includes an obsession that others have a high view of us. It may be a desire to appear wise, or gracious, or a competent

16. à Kempis, *Imitation of Christ*, I.6.2.

leader, or responsible, or fun. This fascination only leads us to despair, for we are constantly trying to maintain a positive image. "Don't have your peace depend on what others might say about you," Thomas à Kempis writes. "Whether they interpret your actions rightly or wrongly, you are still who you are. . . . The person who is neither eager to please others nor afraid to displease them is the one who will enjoy great peace."[17] What matters is living a life of holy integrity rather than making it appear as if we are holy. People in ministry often struggle with this approval disease, due to the many demands placed upon them by well-intentioned parishioners. When pastors' eyes are on the horizon rather than on the clouds, they're seeking approval from those who are below rather than who is above. This view makes it difficult for them to direct the souls of those in their flocks.

Avoiding Spiritual Achievement

Another obstacle that keeps us from prayer in the fourth degree is a quest for achievement, even spiritual achievements. Prayer, reading the Scriptures, attending worship, fasting, and other activities are tangible ways we stay connected with God. In our misunderstanding of the role of these spiritual disciplines in our lives, we falsely believe that our relationship with Christ is in our own hands. Although it has been a word that has been useful to Christians worldwide for many years, I advocate that we retire the term *spiritual disciplines* in favor of the more historic phrase, *means of grace.* A spiritual discipline refers to a routine or a skill that becomes a habit in our lives. We become the actor, and God the intended receiver of our spiritual activities. The entire enterprise becomes yet another example of *incurvatus in se.* We begin with a spiritual activity, we direct it to God, and we expect God to return to us a blessing of spiritual growth.

By making these holy habits a consistent part of our daily activity, we strive (explicitly or implicitly) to sustain our relationship with God and to demonstrate our faithfulness. The habitual inclusion of spiritual disciplines in our lives might be beneficial to us, but in the words of Jean-Baptist Chautard, "there is little genuine inner life . . . in this soul which has . . . a certain number of good habits . . ."[18] The temptation of focusing on a "discipline" or of developing a "holy habit" is superficiality. A change in outward behavior does not necessarily equate to a change in internal disposition. Even a

17. à Kempis, *Imitation of Christ,* III.28.2.

18. Chautard, *The Soul of the Apostolate,* 75.

spiritual habit can become not only a hindrance to our life of prayer, but can actually do damage to our souls.[19] For those among us in pastoral or other expressions of ministry, our very ministerial activities can become hindrances to us. St. Bernard wrote to Pope Eugenius III that he prayed the pope would not succeed in getting through all of his pontifical duties only to find that his heart had become hardened.[20] An indifferent, hardened heart is a real possibility for anyone striving to maintain the spiritual disciplines. This can happen when we schedule times with God in our daily calendar rather than blanketing times with God over our daily calendar.

Conversely, the term *means of grace* refers to a focus on ways of experiencing God's grace. For example, we pray because it orients our lives in a way that allows God to speak to us most clearly. John Wesley described the means of grace as "channels" of God's grace. The focus is not on our own spiritual growth, but on our life paralleling God's life and our will aligning with God's will. This life realignment is not for ourselves, but so that we might become a light in the world. Reading Scripture, for example, merely for the historical information we receive or to study the poetry of the Psalms is quite different from reading Scripture formationally.[21] Instead, our reading of Scripture should, in the words of Michael Casey, "serve as a guide to a more Christlike manner of acting and reacting."[22] Reading God's Word, praying, fasting, worship, or any of the means of grace lead us away from ourselves and into the lives of others. Since God is love and God's love for us is a selfless love, the Holy Spirit uses these means of grace to lead us into the lives of others and away from ourselves.

Our quest for achievement can distract us from what is most important in our lives. Is it more important that we read Scripture or that we get something out of Scripture? In the familiar passage in Luke 10 of Jesus at Mary and Martha's home, Jesus does not condemn Martha's flurry of activities that would become a blessing to Jesus and his disciples. Instead, he said that Mary had discerned the one necessary thing: To sit at the feet of Jesus. In the Latin Vulgate, this term is the *unum necessarium*: the one necessary thing. Living in the fourth degree of prayer is to know without any doubt what that *unum necessarium* is in our lives. Whether we are active in ministry or sitting passively in contemplative prayer, knowing what is

19. Wesley, Sermon XVI, 188.
20. Bernard, *Five Books on Consideration*, II.3.
21. Mulholland, *Shaped by the Word*.
22. Casey, *Grace on the Journey to God*, 143.

indispensable in our lives is the seminal factor in avoiding the achievement factor in a life of prayer.

The Spiritual Danger of Impatience

"For God alone my soul waits in silence, for my hope is from him." Danger lurks in these words from Psalm 62:5, for it may be difficult for many of us to read them with honest authenticity. This verse may not have been as difficult for us if the psalmist David had inserted the word "impatiently" after the word "waits." Impatience is another obstacle to life in the fourth degree of prayer, particularly if we are tempted by spiritual achievement. Before I married into a partly Italian family, I was content with pasta sauce out of a jar. It was quick, convenient, tasty, and filling. When I met my future wife's Italian mother, however, my pasta sauce worldview completely changed. It took her all day to prepare her sauce. What began as stewed tomatoes, cloves of garlic, fresh herbs, hand grated Parmigiano-Reggiano cheese, and homemade meatballs became a dark red simmering masterpiece eight hours later. A life of prayer requires patience as the Holy Spirit lovingly ministers to us, creating in us a masterpiece that will become nourishing spiritual fruit in the lives of others.

Naturalists tell us that when we enter a forest, it takes upwards of forty-five minutes before we can actually feel as if we are part of that environment. Similarly, a life in the fourth degree of prayer takes time for our bodies, spirits, and soul to acclimate. Spending a weeklong retreat at a monastery does not represent a monastic lifestyle. It takes years for the Holy Spirit to prepare us for the spiritual transformation necessary to live in the fourth degree of prayer. Unlike our desire for faster Internet speeds, quicker, more convenient meal preparation, and the most efficient highway route the GPS on our smartphone can find, when we relinquish control of our lives to God, the rate of our spiritual growth is not our concern anymore. As is commonly said, the journey is as important as the destination. According to Luke 17:21, our destination is already inside us: faithful living in the kingdom of God. Our holy living, empowered by God's holy touch on our souls, becomes the spiritual fruit that can become a blessing to others.

Confession Time

Sometimes we find it difficult to live into this fourth degree of prayer due to the culmination of all of these obstacles into one big obstacle: unrepentant sin. Sin is the topic we have no problem addressing, as long as the focus is on someone else. However, unrepentant sin festers like an internal wound in our lives, ever worsening in ways we cannot see but through evidence on the surface of our lives. When we invite God into all the rooms and closets of our spiritual home, we rummage through them with God—sometimes in fear of what we might find in ourselves that we have purposefully forgotten. By not seeking forgiveness for the sins in our lives, we block ourselves from obtaining the spiritual wisdom God desires to impart in our lives. However, we demonstrate wisdom in part in the very act of confessing our sins to God. Bernard of Clairvaux writes, "Sober wisdom is in repentance for past sins, in contempt for present comforts, and in longing for future rewards."[23] We repent for our sins of the past. We also repent for our present love of anything not from God. Finally, we repent for seeking a future that places our own wants at the forefront of our lives. Through the forgiveness of repentant sin, made possible by the salvific life, death, and resurrection of Jesus, the Holy Spirit invites us to this new life of seeing the world and others divinely, rather than humanly.

Perhaps another way of describing life in the fourth degree of prayer is by considering the inverse of a common statement about Christian faith. I believe salvation comes by inviting God to live in our hearts through Jesus Christ by the Holy Spirit. However, I wonder if a lifelong personal emphasis on this reality can actually form a plateau in our faith. When we invite God to take residence in our life, the focus is on *our* life. If we are to take seriously Paul's illustration in Colossians 3 that Christ is our life, I wonder if as disciples of Jesus our focus is on the wrong life: we desire for God to come into our life when instead we should pursue God's life becoming our life.

Living in God

In his 1989 release *Avalon Sunset*, musician Van Morrison describes this hypothesis beautifully. It comes from a song that is more of a modern-day psalm than a pop tune. "When Will I Ever Learn to Live in God" describes a life in which we live in God rather than God living in us. Of course, these

---

23. Bernard, *Monastic Sermons*, 15.4.

two ideas are not mutually exclusive. To live in God presupposes that God is first living in us. In the fourth degree of prayer, as our life becomes God's life and our desires become God's desires, we live in God because God is our life completely instead of God being a part of our life. This allows us to live in the fourth degree of prayer if we're on a silent retreat, in a complex board meeting, or in the middle of a crowd in New York City. As Paul states in Philippians 4:7, the peace that surpasses all human understanding will guard your hearts and minds like a military sentinel from an invasion of the world, no matter where we might find ourselves. As Van Morrison sings repetitively in his song, when will we ever learn? When the nature of our relationship with God fluctuates like the daily tides or like unexpected changes in our emotions, I wonder if we're trying to fit God into our lives instead of surrendering ourselves so we might live in God's life. Again, when will we ever learn?

6

Unintentional Prayer

IN THE YEAR 540, Rome was in decline. The empire was divided in two. The eastern emperor, Justinian, had just reconquered Italy. The Lombards were invading from the north. The centralized government in Rome was ineffective, the once-great Roman Senate had no real power, and local despots took advantage of citizens' property and rights. Because the Roman Senate was obsolete, the papacy assumed civic responsibilities in order to keep order in the streets.

The year 540 was also the year when a wealthy family in Rome had a child they named Gregory. The family held properties in Rome, the Italian countryside, and in Sicily, and was highly respected in the Roman world. Two popes were in Gregory's ancestry, and his family had a reputation for possessing a devout faith in Christ. Gregory would be well-educated, with legal training. However, as he grew, his great desire and perceived calling was to leave society and become a monk. Upon his father's death, Gregory turned the family estate on Rome's Caelian Hill into a monastery, which he called St. Andrews, and where he wished to live out his days in contemplative prayer and peace as a priest.

In 579, however, Pope Pelagius II saw something in Gregory that would be helpful to Rome. He appointed Gregory as the legate in Constantinople. In this role, in which he served as Rome's ambassador, Gregory became a lobbyist, petitioning to Constantinople's leadership the great needs of Rome. He was thankful to be recalled to Rome in 585 and immediately returned to his monastery, where he was elected abbot. However, just four years later Gregory was elected pope as Gregory I, an office he assumed unwillingly at age fifty.

As pope, Gregory found himself responsible for not only facing the sacred responsibilities of the position, but primarily the civic ones. He quickly discovered that he was responsible for paying the daily food rations for imperial solders. He oversaw the repair of Roman aqueducts, secured enough grain for the populace, and engaged in military peacemaking. Although he longed for the simplicity of life at St. Andrews, Gregory was beloved during his papacy for his gentle, reasoned approach to the many difficulties facing Rome. This complicated life was a far cry from his days as a monk on his family's estate. He had entered the priesthood to engage in sacred matters, but was now serving as a skilled administrator, spiritual leader, and the de facto governor of Rome. Gregory poured what time he had in this busy life into writing practical texts on pastoral theology, as well as biblical commentaries and homilies. He wrote nearly 1,000 letters that document his papacy, and which shed light on his personal life. Due to the sanctity of his personal life and both the pastoral ministry and civic executive functions as pope, Gregory was canonized immediately following his death in 604.

Gregory longed for a life that prayed for the world rather than one that was in the midst of the world. However, his capacity to serve Rome so capably and with such grace came from the nature of his soul, which had bound itself to God. The Holy Spirit, so active in his interior life, extended outwardly through his exterior life. Gregory was able to face the many temptations, dangers, and complexities of the political world because his life exhibited the holy life described many centuries later by Chautard: "In the midst of weariness and suffering . . . the saint has nothing to do but abandon himself to the Divine action; otherwise he would be unable to bear the torments . . . intended to bring his perfection to full maturity."[1] By the grace of God, we are able to withstand the uncertainties, anxieties, and complexities of our lives when we are able to see with our hearts that God uses the many issues we face in life to bring us into an intimate relationship with him. When we live in communion with God, a life of faithfulness to God becomes effortless, for in this intimacy we find no space between ourselves and God—no matter what our life situation. This closeness with God comes when we accept God's love for us in a vulnerable way, leading us to forsake all the world offers.

---

1. Chautard, *The Soul of the Apostolate*, 90.

Praying Unintentionally

Living in the fourth degree of prayer is a life of unintentional prayer. Prayer becomes unintentional because, as we go about the various activities of life, we fail to realize that our thoughts and actions have in fact become prayers. Such was the life of Gregory. Because the nature of what it means to be human does not change regardless of time or culture, and because the Holy Spirit continues to dwell in our souls, a life of unintentional prayer in the fourth degree is entirely possible for us, irrespective of our state or station in life. Spiritual excuses have no place in our lives in Christ. We may not live in a monastery, but we can still live lives of contemplative peace. Many of us simply choose not to do so. The small decisions we make every day become the compass that guides our hearts. Succumbing to small, alluring breezes keeps us from following the great wind of the Holy Spirit.

As a diabetic, nothing tempts me more than jelly beans. Sneaking just one of these artificially flavored, corn-syrupy treats has a greater affect on me than producing hyperglycemia, however. Sneaking just one, insignificant orange-flavored jelly bean tempts me in other ways. I become fixated on the fleeting pleasures of the taste buds rather than on the eternal blessings of God. My eyes become fixed on the horizons of the world rather than the God of the world. It's been said that St. Francis of Assisi put ashes in his soup so nothing in this world would be pleasing to him except for the presence of God. While this might be extreme, it serves symbolically as a lesson to all of us that if we desire to live in the fourth degree of prayer, our love for the world or the things of the world (1 John 2:15) must become to us like ash-flavored soup: they're in our lives, but only because they have to be in order for us to make it through a day. Nutritionists encourage their clients to see food not as something they enjoy, but as fuel for their bodies.

Let's contextualize this a bit. We could see automobiles as way to enjoy ourselves with heated leather seats, large touch screens, and DVD players to engage the children. We could also see automobiles as a means to get from one place to another. Church buildings could be to us places that attract new people with comfortable seating, available Wi-Fi, free coffee, and enough technology in worship to engage the senses. We could also see them as places for God's people to gather for worship and study. Life in the fourth degree of prayer is to see all the world offers as necessary distractions. Just as we're able to transform the distractions in prayer into prayers themselves, a life in God is one that sees God in every person and sees symbolic connections with God in the ordinary activities and distractions of life. Perhaps the difference in our perspective of the world and the things of this world comes from the source of that perspective, which changes as our lives deepen in God's grace.

Many times when we experience stress, overwork, or loneliness, we seek to ease our tension with "comfort foods." However, what seem to be comforts of this world are not comforts at all, for our solace should come from God alone. What we discover is that the more we are able to withdraw ourselves from the pseudo-comforts of the world, the more consolation we are able to discover in God.[2] In Galatians 6:14, Paul writes of the world being crucified to him, and he to the world. If the world has been crucified to us, why do we long for what the world offers to comfort us? In order for the world to be crucified to us and us to the world, we need freedom from that which the world tells us we deserve or that will comfort us. In a culture in which pleasure is the greatest end, perhaps we need to crucify our desire for pleasurable indulgence. While we can purchase nearly any product imaginable with a few computer clicks and without leaving our homes, the pseudo-comfort of obtaining stuff will always leave us more unsettled in the long run. The freedom from these lies of the world is what Dorotheos of Gaza refers to as "leaving ourselves."[3] We leave ourselves when we die to ourselves so we might live in Christ. Dying to ourselves is not living in a spiritual coma. Dying to ourselves is death. We no longer live, but Christ lives in us (Galatians 2:20).

When Christ is living in us, prayer is unintentional because prayer has become our new natural way of expressing life. People who live in the fourth degree of prayer have a perspective of the world that comes from deep within their souls, where God meets them. This perpetual, inner, divine encounter does not remain hidden, but shines forth as "the love of God [that] is shed abroad in our hearts by the Holy Spirit" (Romans 5:5). When we don't avail ourselves of this life, we become like the young bird who leaves the nest and flies straight into a garage. We have the whole world to explore in Christ, yet we fly into a garage.

Lessons from the Golden Epistle

In 1145, William of St. Thierry composed a letter to the monks of the Carthusian abbey of Mont Dieu in which he beautifully explained his

2. à Kempis, *Imitation of Christ*, III.12.

3. Dorotheos, *Discourses and Sayings*, 85.

understanding of the progression of the Christian soul. Because of its beauty and formational content, it has become known as the "Golden Epistle." William writes that the soul of the committed Christian passes through three phases: the animal stage, the rational stage, and the spiritual stage. Each of us, William writes, finds ourselves in one of these three stages. "Animal people" govern their lives by their bodily senses and emotions. They live for the divine moments in life in which they perceive God in tangible ways: through their emotions, service to others, and for what a life in Christ can do for them. Today, these people might come to worship to experience the presence of God, to be moved by inspiring sermons, and to feel the satisfaction of tithing their income. Their encounter with God begins and ends with their external senses.

"Rational people," William writes, have moved beyond their desire for self-actualization. These are the Christians with a commitment to understanding the Scriptures and discerning right from wrong doctrines and teachings. They seek God by employing their human ability to study the human soul. This knowledge results in a change in their behavior to conform to the teaching and doctrines they believe. Rational people seek a spiritual life. They are saved through their faith in Christ's redeeming work. However, William argues that they are without the capacity for true love of God, for their faith resides in their rational minds. Rational people perceive the world through inner processing and external implications.

Finally, William defines "spiritual people" as those who are led and enlightened by the Spirit of God. They delight in God simply because God is who God is. The Holy Spirit is the agent of this transformation, for spiritual people have realized that nothing they can experience or discern can direct God's Spirit into their lives. The Spirit is the active agent; they are the passive receptors of Christian perfection. Their desire is to be transformed into the same likeness of God's glory, "borrowing glory from that glory, enabled by the Spirit of God."[4] For these individuals, life on earth is a temporary state. Their desire is to forsake their sensual and rational lives for the life of God, in God. Spiritual people, according to William, have a perspective of life that begins and ends with God. Because physical, or temporal, aspects of the world can interfere with their relationship with God, they are to be endured, but not embraced. Spoken prayer and living prayer are merged into one for people in this heightened phase of the soul, for their entire lives become a living, breathing supplication to God.

4. William, *The Golden Epistle*, par. 45.

The Contentment of Simplicity

To attain a life of unintentional prayer, the Holy Spirit is the one who does the heavy lifting; however, we have the capacity to orient our lives in such a way that we are more open to this work of the Holy Spirit. Perhaps the most important way we can create space for the work of the Spirit is through a simplification of our lives. A simplified Christian life is one that is freed from extraneous clutter that interferes with our capacity to be receptive to the work of God in us. A life of Christian simplicity reflects contentment and gratitude for the grace of God. We don't seek what we don't have and we are thankful for where God has brought us thus far in our lives.

The spiritual concept of *stability* is that we are at peace with our current state of being, our station in life, and our existing location. Stability is not wanting more of anything we currently have. Dennis Okholm describes stability as "being faithful where we are—really paying attention to those with whom we live and to what is happening in our common life."[5] Change itself is not a vice! However, when we are always looking for ways to enact change in our lives, we reveal a hidden restlessness that comes from not being content with our life in God. Because God is not enough for us, we pursue the fantasy that never-ending life modifications might bring contentment. The person who exhibits Christian simplicity through stability reflects the deeply settled peace of the Holy Spirit.

The Importance of Theological Grounding

This approach to simplicity is distinctly Christian. For example, one popular concept of simplicity in Buddhism refers to making space in life for that which can bring about an inner awakening, which allows us to be more transparent to ourselves.[6] This is contrary to a Christian approach to simplicity, in which a simplified life allows us to gaze more clearly on God. For Christians, a simplified life exists so Christ might bring a clearer understanding of ourselves, but only by the work of the Holy Spirit to deepen our focus on Christ. Since we are created in the image of God, our souls long to reflect that image in our daily lives. When we think of our lives reflecting the image of an omniscient, omnipresent, and omnipotent

5. Okholm, *Monk Habits for Everyday People*, 91.

6. For a further examination of the ideals of Buddhist simplicity, see Feldman, *The Buddhist Path to Simplicity*.

God, we might see that as being too great and complex for us to emulate. However, God's nature has been seen by some as not being complex, but simple. I'll attempt to summarize the simplicity of God without taking us on a marathon march through a theological swamp. In the *Summa Theologica*, Thomas Aquinas makes an argument based on Augustine that "God is truly and supremely simple."[7] God is simple not in God's attributes, but in God's nature. God is simple because the characteristics of God do not define God's character. For example, God does not consist of love, justice, mercy, and power. Instead, God *is* love, justice, mercy, and power.

Throughout Scripture we see God defined not by what God does, but by who God is. We see this in Exodus 3:14, in which God states "I Am that I Am," not "I Do What I Do." In Isaiah 9:6, the promised Messiah is called "Wonderful Counselor, Mighty God, Everlasting Father, Prince of Peace." These are identifying statements, not functional titles. Similarly, John 4:24 states that "God is spirit," and not that God functions as a spirit. First John 4:8 declares that "God is love," not that God is loving. Lewis Ayers writes that Augustine supported this understanding of the simplicity of God with the very words of the Nicene Creed, which describes God as "Light from Light" and "true God from true God."[8] God's being is not defined by God's activity, for God's nature is distinct from God's characteristics. Were God's identity based in God's innumerable instances of activity in the world, God's nature would be complex. Because God is not defined by functional roles, God's identity as love, for example, affects how God intersects with human history. Chautard brings this back to reality for us: "The entire life of the incarnate Word manifests the essential and uncommunicable perfection of the Godhead: simplicity."[9] Because of God's nature and our creation in God's image, simplicity should be more than an ideal in our lives. Instead of loving others, perhaps we should embody love. Instead of praying, perhaps we should become prayer. While a life of holy simplicity involves more than merely removing clutter from our lives, removing clutter from our lives is a primary step. Perhaps life simplification is one of the most foundational steps we can make for a virtuous holy life.

7. The quote is from Aquinas, *Summa Theologica*, 1a.3.7, in which he states "*Deus vere et summe simplex est.*"

8. Ayers, *Augustine and the Trinity*, 226.

9. Chautard, *The Spirit of Simplicity*, 27–28.

Simplicity as Foundational

Simplifying our lives is more than clearing out our homes with a yard sale. It's a foundational approach to life in which we figuratively remove everything from our lives, leaving just a slab. As we add structure to that base, we are able to imagine rebuilding our lives with only the most important aspects. In 2005, my parents lost their beautiful, waterfront home to Hurricane Katrina. As they made preparations to rebuild, they realized that the ornate details in their pre-Katrina home weren't necessary in their rebuilding. At that point, they were just thankful to be out of their government-supplied trailer home. Their rebuilt home was just as beautiful but was simpler; it had the necessities of a home without expensive décor. Our lives can be the same way. What we think we need we can usually live without. Our misunderstanding of this becomes so extensive that we confuse *needs* with *wants*. Because we can individualize our lives in countless and ridiculous ways, we bring more clutter to our minds and lives when we could be focused on other, more important matters.

In 1098, the Cistercian monastic order began as a reforming movement within the European church. One aspect of this reform was an insistence on simplicity and uniformity. Cistercian buildings had no ornate stained glass. Their buildings were not wonders to the eye. Their diet was about sustenance rather than pleasing the palate. As the landscape allowed, all Cistercian monasteries were uniform in style and structure. This insistence upon simplicity allowed the monks to spend their energies to focus on contemplative prayer rather than on the maintenance of ornamental architecture. We might refer to this as function over fashion. Dressing for fashion, for example, comes from a desire to draw attention to ourselves.

I used to enjoy wearing clothes that were colorful, new, edgy, and conversation-provoking. Perhaps it was a way for my introverted self to live a bit with extroversion. But as I have been open to the working of the Lord in my own life, I've found a freedom in having five pairs of khaki slacks and several plain dress shirts hanging in my closet. My focus has become less on what I wear every day and more on who I will be as Christ's representative every day. When I've shared this with my classes, female students commonly raise the point, "That's easy for guys. Women can't do that." That may be true if we adhere to what the culture around us has to say about how women dress and the number of shoes they have (although I've known men with a dozen or more pairs of shoes!). It becomes nearly impossible to live in the fourth degree of prayer when our focus is on how we look rather than on who we are. The former leads to pride, while the latter leads to an incarnational life of unintentional prayer.

Of course, a simplification of life remains far deeper than the clothes we wear. Simplicity of heart is having one focus of our lives, upon which everything else is based (Matthew 6:33). While we may have a stirring debate regarding trickle-down economics, trickle-down spirituality is biblical truth. When we keep Christ primary in our lives—or at the head of the body of Christ (Colossians 1:18)—everything we do is affected. The Holy Spirit trickles down through, or saturates, all segments of our lives. Rather than having complicated, multiple allegiances, the disciple keeps fidelity to God alone. It really is that simple.

Prayer as All in All

In his important work *A Plain Account of Christian Perfection*, John Wesley suggests that "all that a Christian does, even in eating and sleeping, is prayer, when it is done in simplicity, according to the order of God, without either adding to or diminishing from it by his [or her] own choice."[10] A simple life is a prayerful life, for since we are no longer enamored by the fleeting trends in fashion, social media, and technology, we are left with a greater capacity to perceive the world with holy eyes. Wesley lived what he wrote, for although he could have been a wealthy man, he chose to live modestly and with as few distractions as possible. For many of us, this approach to life seems akin to an overly idealistic ascetic existence. In a world of multitasking, perusing through dozens of emails in an afternoon, and having all the news of the world in our very hands, a simple life seems impossible. Just when we think technology will allow us to streamline the many tasks placed upon us, we're asked to do even more because technology allows us to streamline our many tasks.

Slowing Down without Losing Speed

A few years ago, after I presented a paper at an academic conference on major themes in Bernard of Clairvaux's letters, a graduate student approached me and asked a question I didn't expect: "What would St. Bernard do with email?" Would a reforming, contemplative Cistercian abbot utilize email?

---

10. Wesley, *A Plain Account of Christian Perfection*, 438.

In some ways, the question is impossible to answer, for putting a twenty-first-century worldview on a medieval European is not only unfair but follows a poor historical method. As the student stood there anticipating my answer, I thought for a moment, and then another moment, and then finally responded, "Knowing his personality, I'm thankful Bernard didn't have the option ever to know about email." We have become so accustomed to life at 100 mph that if we go without a capacity to check our email for a few hours, we feel overwhelmed and behind. We can't expect others to adjust their worldview so we might simplify our lives, but by God's grace we do have the capacity to have an awareness of what is important, what can wait, and what we don't need.

Nurturing Complexity in the Body of Christ

Perhaps clergy should take some of the responsibility for hindering simplicity in the lives of those we endeavor to draw closer to God. The modern sanctuary is a prime example. We cannot simply turn the lights on or off, for the dozens of multicolored LED lights are connected to complex mixing boards. Wireless microphones, fast Wi-Fi, and animated video projections are becoming essential aspects of sanctuary construction. For the record, I am no Luddite, intent on resisting new technological advances. I'm thankful for the computer with which I am typing these words, and for the Internet that has been most helpful in my research. My life as a pastor became more efficient when email and smartphones became a reality. My concern with technology in a local church is that we can falsely believe it's necessary for ministry and indispensable for effective worship. Bernard of Clairvaux wrote that many times clergy will construct sanctuaries "to stimulate devotion in carnal people with material ornaments because they cannot do so with spiritual ones."[11] If the gospel we present to people is not attractive enough to draw people to God, then perhaps we're presenting the wrong gospel. The beautiful simplicity of God's salvific love and indwelling of the Holy Spirit can become lost in our attempt to make local church events and facilities the focus of parish life.

When I served as a pastor of a church near the seminary where I taught part-time, a large percentage of our congregation was students. At the time, I used an iPad for my sermon notes. I received the iPad as a gift and found that in preaching it was convenient, saved paper, and I was able

11. Bernard, *Apology to Abbot William*, XII.28.

to tweak my notes easily at the last moment. I noticed, however, that as the weeks and months progressed, more and more seminary students began attending Sunday worship with brand new iPads. Without even realizing it, I was modeling to them that modern preaching required the use of expensive technology. On one memorable Sunday, I addressed the situation directly during worship by apologizing to them for implicitly putting them into debt. The result of my desire to bring simplicity to sermon delivery was a direct, negative consequence on others. Unfortunately, the students perceived that the means of sharing the gospel message coexisted equally with the essential truths of the gospel message itself. As parents of young children know, they pay attention to us with far more detail than we realize. How we present the gospel to others (explicitly or implicitly) can either draw people closer to Christ or away from Christ. A singularly focused life in God can minimize the misunderstandings of a godly life in others.

Well-Intentioned Stress

Perhaps a lack of simplicity in our own lives is more of a reality than we might recognize. I believe this begins with a hesitation to properly present ourselves with authenticity. I've known people so ensnared with the maintenance of how they appear to others that it becomes the focus of their daily life. All this does is bring complexity to our emotions and priorities, which shifts our life-gaze from Christ to ourselves. Other times, we overthink decisions we have to make to avoid making a poor decision. It truly is shocking how much unnecessary stress we place on ourselves all to maintain a positive reputation in the eyes of others. Many times we unnecessarily produce a Rube Goldberg machine in our lives by allowing our emotions or logical processes to take charge. The simple truth that "God is love" becomes lost to us.

Several years ago, a heavily burdened Kevin came to my study in the church office after his therapist had encouraged him to meet with me. Kevin entered my office looking like a man with heavy weights on his shoulders. He had the appearance of someone who was tired, stressed, and desperate. As we talked I discovered that much of his anxiety came from an overwhelming uncertainty about the future. He grieved an exploitation of the earth's natural resources, corruption in the government, violent crime, family and career stress due to a predicted downturn in the economy, and even the state of his favorite college basketball team. Put simply, Kevin was a mess. In fact, I told him he was a mess. His obsession with all of these issues was keeping his eyes off of our God, who is above all of these important concerns.

I took out a blank hourly calendar and we went through his typical day. Every weekday, Kevin woke up and turned on the news. As he drove to work, he listened to the news. On his way to lunch and then home, he listened to talk radio. After putting the kids in bed, he turned on one of the news channels while he perused social media. Kevin was so deep in his anxiety that he couldn't even see the pattern right before his eyes. "How might your day look if you didn't listen to or watch any news?" I asked him. He replied as if I had just asked the daftest question he had ever heard. "Then how in the world would I know what was going on? We have to know what's happening so we can bring about change!" Kevin had invited the anxious complexities of the world into his life, and the world's problems had taken over. He had so allowed the voices, images, and opinions of the modern news media to replace his hope in God that he was left with desperate hopelessness. It took Kevin several weeks before he was able to view the news media with God's eyes rather than with human solutions. Christians have the greatest answer to the world's many issues, and I'm thankful for the hands, feet, and mouths of faithful disciples who engage the culture around us with the light of Christ. In Kevin's situation, however, by his continuous exposure to the world's issues, the darkness of the world was obscuring his perspective.

Internal Peace

We began this chapter with a brief look at the enigmatic life of Gregory I. When the Pope Pelagius II sent him to Constantinople as his *apocrisiarius*, Gregory was asked to leave a life of prayerful contemplation to become the pope's ambassador. Many of us would be honored with such an appointment. However, Gregory was content with what Thomas à Kempis would later refer to as a desire to be unknown and esteemed as nothing, as Gregory seems not to have been interested in titles or honors.[12] He also knew that in this esteemed position he would become embroiled in the world of international politics in a region with disdain for Rome's frequent requests for financial support. However, Gregory trusted God and left for the East,

---

12. à Kempis, *Imitation of Christ*, I.2.4.

knowing that the peace of God would certainly be in Constantinople just as it had been in Gregory's monastic estate.

Gregory was able to enter the precarious political world and find contentment because the peace and stability in his life were internal, not external. He would write, "Solitude of mind is rightly given at first to those turning from the world in order to restrain the clamor of earthly desires rising from within . . . In that silence of the heart, while we keep watch within through contemplation, we are as if asleep to all things that are without."[13] No matter what chaos exists in the world around us, the Holy Spirit brings calm to our minds so we might be able to deal with the stresses of life. The result is that we might live a life of unintentional prayer in the fourth degree no matter the clamor around us. While we can't avoid the obligations and expectations of life, we don't live for those things because our souls aren't attached to them. Gregory didn't write these words from his monastic prayer room, but when he was in the throes of considerable turmoil as pope. The perspective we have of daily obligations and their place in our lives makes all the difference between living in the first or second degree of prayer and the fourth. A certain freedom exists for those of us living in the fourth degree of prayer. When prayer becomes so unintentional that we live and breathe as little prayers to God, the burdens of the world (while certainly not disappearing), seem tempered a bit and not as unwieldy as perhaps they once appeared.

Self-Soothing Isolation

When I was a child, I spent a good deal of time by myself. It's not that I wasn't social, but instead of having many friends like others my age, I had two or three really good friends. When I wasn't with them, I could usually be found in my room either reading books, writing stories, listening to music, or composing little songs on my guitar. I remember spending twenty minutes studying a paragraph from Tolkien, trying to capture exactly what the master author was trying to convey. I listened to songs over and over on my record player to hear every note and try to identify every instrument. I wrote stories about living in different historical times and how that might affect my relationship with God, which was quite real to me. When not at school or with our church family, I would leave my room only when my

---

13. Gregory I, *Morals on the Book of Job*, 30.XI.54.

well-intentioned parents forced me to engage with the real world. To say I was a tad socially awkward would be a fair assessment.

When my world was upended following my parents' divorce, I used my introspective nature as a form of self-soothing from the emotional pain. Rather than risk further hurt, I relied on my individual relationship with God, in whom I could trust without question. I didn't know it at the time, but my desire to remain guarded with others actually became a hindrance to my relationship with Christ. "May God shelter us from the danger of being our own guides," wrote Dorotheos of Gaza.[14] Isolation from others is not part of our historical faith. From the earliest chapters of the Old Testament, we see the importance of community. It was not good for Adam to be alone, so God created Eve (Genesis 2:18). In Exodus 3, God tells Moses that when he goes to the King of Egypt, both the elders of the Hebrews and Moses' brother Aaron will be with him.

The contrast throughout 1 Samuel between King Saul, who isolated himself from others, and David, who surrounded himself with others, is a key distinction in their faithfulness as leaders and servants of God. Psalms were meant to be sung collectively. Prophets were sent by God to counsel God's people. In the New Testament, Jesus surrounded himself with disciples, and when he sent them out, it was never alone. The early Christians in Acts lived together and shared everything. In one of the earliest extrabiblical documents about life in Christian community, Hippolytus of Rome wrote of the relationship between accountability and faithful living in Christian community.[15]

The Painful Beauty of Vulnerability

Certainly, the idea of vulnerable living with other Christians is as ancient to our faith tradition as is the creation of humanity. In fact, our creation in the image of God implies that our communal identity is Trinitarian in nature. The ideal is that we should relate to each other in love as the persons of the Trinitarian Godhead relate to each other. When St. Benedict crafted his *Rule*, and the Cistercian founders later polished it to include accountability between monastic houses, and when Jacob Spener postulated the idea for stoic Lutherans to meet together for prayer and holy conversation, and when John Wesley created band meetings so his Methodists could

14. Dorotheos, *Discourses and Sayings*, 129.

15. Hippolytus, *On the Apostolic Tradition*.

rummage around in each other's souls, they were each building upon the foundation established in Scripture and modeled in the very nature of God himself. We cannot expect to live into the fourth degree of prayer on our own. To attempt such an endeavor would reveal a self-reliant pride, which shows itself in the first degree of prayer.

When the Holy Spirit works in our lives by refining and smelting sin from our lives, the process can be exhausting, even taking a physical toll on us. In the late nineteenth century, a successful, well-loved pastor and evangelist experienced this very situation. Henry Clay Morrison was the pastor of one of the oldest Methodist congregations in Kentucky. The people in Danville loved their pastor. The church was growing, people were coming to faith in Christ, and his preaching was electric. Yet unbeknownst to the congregation, Morrison was experiencing the most difficult year of his life. During one particular two-week time, he experienced fainting spells, midnight terrors, and restless midnight walks through the streets of the city. On one occasion, while walking in the town square, he stumbled, fainted, and had to be carried home by townspeople. Morrison said of this experience, "It would hardly be lawful for me to go into details and tell what the Lord revealed to me of the nature of sin, and hatefulness of it. He so withdrew all comfort from me and all witness of acceptance, that I had a foretaste of what it would be to be separated from Him forever. In addition Satan buffeted, ridiculed, taunted, and tempted me almost beyond endurance."[16]

It was not another Methodist preacher, his bishop, or a church member who became the voice of God to Morrison. It was a local Presbyterian minister. This professor of Calvinist theology assisted Morrison in his spiritual battle and encouraged the Methodist evangelist that the Holy Spirit was indeed at work in his life, purging him from sin and preparing him for the next phase of life with God. Because the people God brings to us are sometimes unexpected, it's important for us to have a healthy awareness and openness to input from the most unlikely of sources. When these disturbing spells ceased, Morrison had a clear vision of the calling of God, which lasted the remainder of his life on earth.

When the Holy Spirit transitions us into the fourth degree of prayer, we may not experience physical symptoms like Henry Clay Morrison did. Each of us reacts differently to the movement of the Holy Spirit. God knows which areas of our lives need to be purified in his holy smelting pot. Perhaps Morrison (who would spend the rest of his life as a traveling revival

16. Wimberly, *A Biographical Sketch of Henry Clay Morrison*, 97–98.

preacher, college president, seminary founder, and world evangelist) experienced these physical symptoms of the work of the Holy Spirit in his life to remind him that only by God's strength and the support of others would he have the physical strength to be the faithful disciple God had called him to be. A writer may experience a divinely timed writer's block to remind her that every word she types is by the grace of God alone. Whatever the means, this spiritual purgation is a gift of God to purify and remind us that it is impossible to live in the fourth degree of prayer by our own strength. Unintentional prayer is impossible to attain on our own and inconceivable to maintain by our own strength. It requires a willing submission to God, an openness to the ministry of others in our life, and the humility to acknowledge that we are incapable of persevering on our own steam.

When We Stop Trying, the Holy Spirit Moves

We must be patient with ourselves. The reality of a life of unintentional prayer is that at times we find a life of prayer ebbing and flowing like waves on a beach. When the Apostle Paul refers to a life that has been set free from sin in Romans 6:18, he doesn't mean that we have been made sinless. As human beings, we still have a sinful nature. The difference is that for the person striving for holy living in the fourth degree of prayer, sin becomes the exception in our lives. We cease focusing on trying not to sin and instead live with holy abandon. When we do find ourselves placing more attention on life's distractions than we ought, this acknowledgement could actually be a blessing to us, and a gift of grace from God. Thomas Merton writes that it's in these times of perceived weakness that we "realize our dependence on God and to receive at every moment God's grace."[17] If we're not famished, we don't realize the importance of food. Paul writes that when we are weak, Christ is strong (2 Corinthians 12:10). Our strength comes from God's strength, who by the Holy Spirit sustains, empowers, and keeps us close to the heart of Christ. This is true whether we are in early morning private prayer, driving to work in heavy traffic, or shopping for groceries. This is the essence of unintentional prayer: it's a constant awareness of living, working, breathing in the presence of God; an orientation of life in which the Holy Spirit gives our spiritual eyes new lenses through which we see the world.

17. Merton, "On Prayer."

Hildegard of Bingen uses the imagery of flight to describe this life orientation. Because the Lord God has given us spiritual wings with which to fly, by the Holy Spirit we are able to take wing and pass swiftly and gracefully over what Hildegard calls "the poisonous and deadly things" of the world.[18] This is similar to an image of her contemporary, Bernard of Clairvaux, who wrote that the monastic life is like a bridge over a lake that leads one to heaven. One could swim through the lake to get there, but the voyage of life for the holy person is walking above the murky water of the world on a holy bridge.[19]

No Prescription Needed

As you have probably noticed, our discussion has shied away from a step-by-step approach to this life. A simple rationale is that life in the fourth degree of prayer is not prescriptive. Because each of us is a beloved, unique creation of God, we each have different purgative issues. A generalized, step-by-step process for spiritual growth is simply impossible to formulate. Were it only that easy! As we grow to know ourselves uniquely as God has created us and are able to submit our lives to the risen Christ, God reveals to us the wonder of a life in God, enlivened by the Holy Spirit. How this happens is as unique as each person God has created in his image. I like to think that the Holy Spirit's personalization of this process is another sign of God's love for each one of us—a grace reminding us of the precious rarity of the individual human soul. While we cannot achieve this on our own, we do have a small role to play. In his poem "Spring Morning," author and poet A. A. Milne unwittingly described our activity in this Holy Spirit process:

> If you were a bird, and lived on high,
> You'd lean on the wind when the wind came by,
> You'd say to the wind when it took you away:
> "That's where I wanted to go today!"[20]

When we lean on the wind of the Holy Spirit, the Lord takes us to places in our life we might never have dreamed we could go. Our primary responsibility is to leave the comfort of the nest and fall into the care of

18. Hildegard, *Scivias*, 4.1.2.

19. Bernard, *Monastic Sermons*, 35. This image is reminiscent of Isaiah 35:8, which refers to the "highway of holiness."

20. This poem is found in Milne, *When We Were Very Young*, 37.

God. Only then will we realize that the life we've always yearned to live is in God, wherever he may place us, and wherever the wind of the Holy Spirit takes us. This is the life of unintentional prayer.

7

Life in the Eternals

SHE SAT IN HER wheelchair at the dark end of the hall, nearly hidden from everyone else. In fact, she was so far down the corridor I had trouble discerning if anyone was there at all. It was November 1992 and my second week as a student chaplain at the nursing home. So far, I relished opportunities to bring joy to these frail residents at this nicely appointed residential community. But as I approached her wheelchair to greet the resident I hadn't yet met, I froze when my eyes met hers. Through the unlit corner of the hall, I could discern dark, leathery skin that covered her frail bones. Her knotted hair fell like a tangled web on her shoulders. Whether it was fear of not wanting to offend her or simple intimidation, I vainly searched for rationale why I should not approach her and not move on to the next, less frightening resident. I could find none.

Resolved to action, I stepped forward with caution, not knowing if this brittle human being would be able to hear or see me. I squinted my eyes to make contact with her in the dark hallway when I was startled by what seemed to be a bright light. It was her eyes. As they made contact with mine, all of my intimidating fear scattered. Her countenance increasingly lit the hallway and she revealed a large, toothy smile. "Hello," she whispered in a graveled voice. I introduced myself to her as a seminary student serving as a student chaplain for the next semester. "I'm . . . right . . . here . . . every . . . day," she whispered with steady determination.

Clemmie was the only African American resident in the nursing home. She looked old for her eighty-seven years. Every Monday for the following twelve weeks I met with her at the end of the hall. Our time together was so regular that the nurses had a chair ready for me when I arrived on Monday mornings. Clemmie's luminous eyes had witnessed pain, joy, oppression, victory, poverty, wealth, and loneliness. She had experienced the death of two husbands, three children, and most of her extended family. She had no one to visit her, no shoulders for her tears, no arms to embrace her body's brittle frame. Yet in Clemmie I met a woman of God who was never alone. Her realization of God's tangible presence was a faith I had only discovered in the writings of holy Christians who had lived hundreds of years earlier. Clemmie's scratchy, quiet voice became the voice of the Savior to me. I learned of her lifelong trust in God, of her hope of a new future freed from her arthritis-inflicted body, her loving service to others (including to those who had mistreated her), and her ministry of prayer that continued to this very day. She knew the names of all the nurses and staff, their personal struggles, and the state of their relationships with God. Clemmie nourished me with uneducated wisdom my brilliant seminary professors simply couldn't offer. In her mind, God had blessed her beyond measure: she had a bed, three meals a day, shelter from the elements, and all day long to give thanks to God by shining his light into the lives of others. "I got nobody, but I got Everybody," she would say.

On my final Monday at the nursing home, I found Clemmie in her regular location at the dark end of the hall, praying for everyone who shuffled by. I recollected my first fearful encounter with her, intimidated by the frail creature before me. Now she had become a messenger from God who regularly filled my life with nourishing spiritual fruit. I held her hand and explained that my semester of ministry practicum was coming to a close. Clemmie's eyes made contact with mine and she whispered slowly, "You'll know where to find me in God's big house. I'll be there." To this day I can't discern if my tears were the indication of sorrow, joy, or a blending of both. When I returned to visit Clemmie after Christmas holiday, she was gone. The nurses said they discovered her lifeless body in her bed the day after Christmas. Since they couldn't find any family, she was laid to rest at Evergreen Memory Gardens by the citizens of Fayette County, Kentucky. I ended a poem about her with these words:

> Clemmie, O Clemmie!
> Alone in this world but never alone.
> You have no one but you have Everyone
> St. Clemmie of Darby

Clemmie exhibited the ideals of a life in the fourth degree of prayer. Prayer in the fourth degree is a life without regard for oneself. In a Christian culture that centers on personal growth and other manifestations of spiritual hedonism, life in the fourth degree seems to be the exception these days. The primary reason for this is clear: many Christians have too much interest having the right answer, having the largest TV on the block, the most successful congregation, or memorizing the most Scripture. Our fascination with improving ourselves in any way demonstrates our self-absorption and spiritual emptiness. Whereas Jesus tells us to deny ourselves (Matthew 16:23), we spend time engaging in what 1 John 2:16 describes as the "lust of the flesh, the lust of the eyes, and the pride of life." Many of us who have surrendered our lives to Christ are still living from our five senses rather than from our soul. Certainly, we live in bodies. God has blessed us with physical senses so we might engage and celebrate the world around us. However, living in our body is poles apart from living in the flesh.

Having a Faithful Focus

The worldly ideals of self-improvement have no place in the life of the disciple of Jesus. Conversely, a life surrendered to Christ and filled with the Holy Spirit has one desire: faithfulness to God. Perhaps this faithfulness is best described by Jesus himself in Matthew 22:37–39, when he summarized the two greatest commandments as 1) loving God with all our heart, all our mind, and all our strength, and 2) loving our neighbor as ourselves. Each of these commandments is impossible without the other. Without the first commandment, we cannot have an understanding of ourselves that permits us to love ourselves or others. Without the second commandment, the first describes a solitary life removed from others, which is the antithesis of incarnational living. Our pursuit of God, self-awareness, knowledge, or any other ideal should never remain with ourselves. Instead, the whole of our lives should lead us out of ourselves and into the lives of others.

In his thirty-sixth sermon on the Song of Songs, Bernard of Clairvaux affirms a person's quest for knowledge of God and self-awareness, but cautions not to replace the means with the end. He writes:

> There are some who long to know for the sole purpose of knowing, and that is shameful curiosity; others who long to know in order to become known, and that is shameful vanity . . . There are others still who long for knowledge in order to sell its fruits for money or honors, and this is shameful profiteering; others again who long to know in order to be of service, and this is charity. Finally there

are those who long to know in order to serve themselves, and this is prudence.[1]

While some scholars have characterized this twelfth-century abbot as an anti-academic, Bernard's opposition to the growing rise of universities in France had to do with the abuse of knowledge rather than of obtaining knowledge itself. If we seek educational pursuits or a deeper understanding of Scripture to bolster our reputation or further our career, we've engaged in a selfish endeavor. However, using our acquisition of knowledge for the betterment of ourselves and others leads to wisdom and love. I often remind my seminary students that their education to prepare for ministry is not about the pursuit of a good grade, a diploma, or to have degree abbreviations behind their name. That might suffice for other graduate programs, but for those called to ministry, their academic preparation in theology, biblical studies, preaching, and missiology is not for themselves, but for all the people they will encounter in ministry in the decades ahead. For the most part, congregants care little about what grade their pastor received in systematic theology. Yet I am astounded at students who focus so intently on making a high grade that they lose sight of how a particular course might equip them for ministry. If we truly love God to the depths that are available to human beings on earth, the pursuits of our lives must culminate in love. It's simply impossible to love God without loving others. We don't seek a blessing or personal benefit in our holy pursuits, but with the right life alignment, God gifts us in ways we can't even describe.

Having the Right Gauge

We live in a world of measurements: academic grades, corporate profits, voter counts, world records of all sorts, athletic statistics, and others. Our consistent exposure to these cultural gauges creeps into our relationship with Christ. Stated simply, we cannot measure spiritual growth. Unlike the visible changes of our human bodies over time, our spiritual lives are not the same way. As we're each created in the image of God, we have a soul that is unseen except by God. Our soul is what connects us with God. Rather than attempting to articulate spiritual growth that takes place throughout our lives, perhaps we should refer to spiritual deepening. Even though we can't see the process, the roots of a plant mature deeply into the soil in order

1. Bernard, *Sermons on the Song of Songs*, 36.3.

to bring health and stability to the plant. We can see evidence of healthy roots by the health of the plant above the ground. A congregation that measures its success by its worship numbers, membership, or giving may be no more healthy than a tree recently planted in a thin layer of sandy soil. You might admire the tree for awhile, but it will not be able to produce fruit or even survive because its unseen roots are not secured in healthy soil. As one wise monk shared with me, "A holy life isn't following a route on a spiritual map. It's to have the map and walk in it without fear of losing your way."

Chautard writes that the Holy Spirit uses our interior lives to enable effective ministry in our exterior lives: "Action relies upon contemplation for its fruitfulness; and contemplation, in turn, as soon as it has reached a certain degree of intensity, pours out upon our active works some of its overflow."[2] Both contemplation (our internal lives) and action (our external lives) are essential for discipleship. When these two are united by the Holy Spirit, the fourth degree of prayer becomes realized in us. The fires of Holy Spirit zeal hidden deep in our hearts ignites the lives of those around us, potentially without us even realizing that it's happening. It's this union of the internal and the external, the contemplation and the action, that comprises a life in the fourth degree of prayer.

One way to assess spiritual deepening is by the evidence of the Fruit of the Spirit in one's life. As listed in Galatians 5, Paul presents love, joy, peace, long-suffering, gentleness, goodness, faith, meekness, and self-control as a single fruit, not many. They all work together to produce spiritually nutritious food for others, offered through the holiness of our own lives. For many years, I regularly met with a group of men in the congregation I served in order to help each other recognize the evidence of spiritual fruit in our lives. These biweekly noon gatherings were not always pleasant lunch meetings! Out of our deep love for one another, we met for group spiritual direction by assessing the evidence of spiritual fruit in us. The focus was not on outward behavior or emotions, but on deep, unseen health in each other's souls. We didn't dwell on how many days in the past week we prayed, read Scripture, etc. Instead, we investigated the state of each other's souls. I suppose we followed a modified version of John Wesley's rules for his band societies, written in 1738. We willingly invited others to dig into our souls and rummage around for anything we might be hiding from them. This sounds insensitive, but it was done out of holy love for another, and not to incite shame or embarrassment.

2. Chautard, *The Soul of The Apostolate*, 59.

Christians who live outside of authentic Christian community are no better than what Benedict of Nursia calls *sarabaites*.[3] They are Christians who live outwardly Christian lives but only for show. They have no one to guide them in the life of sanctity. Because they have no spiritual compass of community, they wander aimlessly through life, calling holy whatever they deem to be holy. They change the rules of morality and theology as it pleases them because they do not need the Holy Spirit to offer honest, hard-love input from others. Life in the fourth degree of prayer has no thought of an island identity. Rather, it is one that lives harmoniously with other disciples of Jesus in an authentic spiritual family (Matthew 12:50).

Faithfulness and Diversity

Whether it's being obedient to monastic vows in a community removed from society, participating in a classic Wesleyan band meeting, engaging in a weekly prayer meeting, or some other formative community experience, what matters most is that we engage people in our lives so we might be a blessing to them. Desert father Abba Poemen said, "If three people meet, of whom the first full-preserves interior peace, and the second gives thanks to God in illness, and the third serves with a pure mind, these three are doing the same work."[4] The Christian family is a richly diverse body, each community and individual serving a necessary role. St. Benedict didn't have all the answers; nor did Martin Luther, John Wesley, or any one or any other reforming or restoring tradition. We must resist the temptation to impersonate another person or another approach to God. Jean Pierre de Caussade wrote, "Different souls cannot lay claim to the same mixture of virtues, or to the same experience that others have, but all can be united to God, all can be surrendered to His holy purpose, all can receive the touch best suited for them . . ."[5]

Living Your Life

I wish I had read this in Caussade before I graduated from seminary. You may remember in chapter 4 that I shared the influence of my professor, Dr.

3. Benedict, *Rule*, ch. 1.
4. Ward, ed., *The Sayings of the Desert Fathers*, 171.
5. Cassaude, *Abandonment to Divine Providence*, 2.V.

Jerry Mercer, on my life. I thought Mercer was the holiest man I knew. I wanted to emulate Mercer in every way possible so I might be holy, as well. After graduation, I found my first pastoral appointment to be a spiritual desert. No longer was I in a community that remained singularly focused on the things of God. I was in a local church whose members saved God conversation for Sundays and Wednesdays. Their focus seemed to be on other topics. Holy conversations with Mercer about nuances in Christian spirituality became memories. I tried filling my office with incense, but after an incident with the local fire department, I decided it would be prudent not to attempt that again. I suppose Jerry's office didn't have a smoke alarm wired to the nearest fire station, like my new one did. Below is an excerpt from one of the poems I wrote during this period:

> Alone in a strange new world,
> Grasping to keep afloat
> In this great ocean of possibilities.
> Searching for the meaning of why I'm here.
>
> I know nothing.
> I'm a dimming flame at the end of a vanishing wick.
> Mercerian courage gone forever.

I remember calling Professor Mercer one afternoon. Perhaps the mere sound of his voice would snap me out my spiritual funk. I explained to him the wilderness state of my soul because I missed our conversations of saints and trips to Gethsemani Abbey. After I whined for a few minutes, I awaited his usually joyful and comforting voice. He replied with six words: "Mike, my brother, I've failed you." He then abruptly ended the call. For several weeks I wondered why my spiritual mentor hung up on me.

One afternoon, as I read a sermon by John Wesley, I understood Mercer's candid response. Wesley wrote, "What we do has an immediate effect on those around us. Don't be a distraction in their life that takes their focus off of God."[6] Mercer thought he had failed me because I desired to be like him and not like Jesus. God has created us to commune with him in Jesus. We need not try to be someone else in our prayers. Prayer in the fourth degree should always come from the core of our souls as we are, and not in the persona of someone else or in some other stage of spiritual life we desire to be.

6. Wesley, Sermon CXL, 504.

Living in the fourth degree of prayer should be according to the way God has created each one of us. Put plainly, to emulate the spiritual practices of someone else is to engage in idolatry. Some of us are uncomfortable with burning incense. Others are uncomfortable with deep sharing in a Wesleyan band. As Caussade wrote, we can be united to God even though we employ different means. For some in the body of Christ, their calling is to live in the midst of society so as to introduce Christ to those who no idea who Christ is. Others are called to a more hidden vocation, praying for the ones who are representing Christ out on the busy streets. Life in the fourth degree of prayer does not look like one particular spiritual approach or calling. The Apostle Paul's description of this in 1 Corinthians 12 is an example of the importance of diversity in the body of Christ. As one monk shared with me, "As we live and pray behind these [monastery] walls, we're the part of the body of Christ that's below the skin." When Paul writes in 1 Thessalonians 5:17 to "pray without ceasing," the apostle does not specify the *how* of this endless prayer. He merely exhorts the church in Thessalonica to interact with God unceasingly.

A Kingdom Identity

Perhaps what enables continuous prayer is a worldview that facilitates prayerful living. As people of the kingdom of God, we're called to have priorities, interests, and perspectives that are different than people outside of God's kingdom. We sometimes forget that our primary citizenship is not in any nation on earth, but in the kingdom of God. We're called to see the world through God's eyes rather than through nationalistic eyes. Allegiance to a certain political party or movement in the hope that it can solve a country's social ills is a secular mind-set. This thinking is, in fact, the opposite of Christian hope, for placing our trust in human endeavors or institutions will always lead to disappointment.

Let's be clear: a focus on citizenship in the kingdom of God does not make Christians anarchists. In Mark 12:17, Jesus makes a clear statement that the emperor has a role in the world and that under legal duty his followers should be obedient. However, Jesus also says that we owe God our spiritual allegiance. A separation exists here between the rule of humanity and the rule of God. When in vain we attempt to bring these two together, we can inadvertently confuse which ruler governs which realm.

Paul's deference for political authorities in Romans 13 and 1 Timothy 2 indicates a respect for governmental authorities and a place for them in God's earthly rule. In the latter example, the apostle exhorts Timothy to offer multiple prayers for everyone, including kings and rulers, that the followers of Christ might lead peaceful and quiet lives, undisturbed by the governmental authorities. Paul does not encourage Timothy to pray that God raises Christians into powerful political positions in the Roman Empire. Instead, he prays the authorities would leave the Christians alone. Paul's focus is not on engaging the world of politics with a Christian worldview, but for Christians to engage the world with the light of Christ. This does not mean we ignore the injustices of government, however.

Throughout history, Christians have stood for those who have no voice. We become confused, however, when we believe that human laws or Christians in political power will solve societal injustices. The example we have in Scripture and in the early church is that the followers of Jesus lived without political power or influence and were undeservedly tortured, yet they prayed for boldness and to be a missiological witness. Alan Kreider, referring to the writings of Lactantius (250–325), describes how these primitive Christians desired to be martyrs because the horror of their executions would so offend the moral sensibilities of the pagan Roman witnesses that they would convert to Christianity.[7] Rather than seeking legislation to prohibit Christian executions, the early Christians focused on representing Christ well in their public deaths. In their attempt to extinguish the grass fires of the Christian movement through public persecutions and executions, the entire Empire became aflame.

This perspective of the Christian life is all but extinct in the Christian West. The early church had an eternal perspective of life, which is indicative of people living in the fourth degree of prayer. Life is not just what we experience with our senses. Life is eternal. When the emphasis of our lives is on our pre-death existence, we fail to grasp the anthropological foundation of our humanity. We perpetuate a life-vision that is limited to an earthly existential reality rather than the timelessness of our reality. Many years ago, I led a children's worship service in our congregation. Our goal was twofold: 1) introduce children to Christ, and 2) teach them how to worship God. We believed the goal of children's ministry in a local church should be to prepare them for the next stage of life: participation in youth ministry. When I became a youth pastor, my task was to prepare the teenagers for

7. Kreider, *The Patient Ferment of the Early Church*, 34.

a life of discipleship as a young adult. As adults, are we allowing the Holy Spirit to prepare ourselves for life after our life on earth? Having an eternal view of life shifts the focus of our lives from what is happening now to what is happening in the future. An eternal life perspective allows us to live incarnationally in the world as true representatives of Christ. Our priorities reflect this view of life. The result is a lack of desire for all the world offers because we know it is fleeting.

An Eternal Perspective

As a pastor, I was privileged to be with individuals during their final breaths of earthly life. It's an honor to be with these saints as they die. It was a greater blessing to have opportunities to help them prepare for leaving this earth, reminding them that death is merely a changeover into a new life. When we have an eternal perspective of life, the death of a loved one can have a shade of joy, for we know they still exist, only in the presence of God where we will one day join them in the great cloud of witnesses (Hebrews 12:1). In death, life doesn't end. It merely transitions.

For some of us, having an eternal perspective seems impossible, for how can we have perception of that which we have not experienced? We can read about what has happened in the past, but all we know is the here and now—the future too seems too speculative to comprehend. Perhaps many of us cannot fathom having an eternal perspective of human life because we are so consumed with the present world. We focus on careers, reputations, obtaining that which we think we deserve, and living a comfortable lifestyle. We arm ourselves with personal weapons so we might defend ourselves from physical harm or death (as if death for a Christian is something to avoid at all costs!). This approach to life exhibits life in the first or second degree of prayer. It's a life of never-ending anxieties and worry. In fact, this limited horizontal attitude of life exhibits nihilism, for we can't face the thought of not living on earth.

Seeing Between the Spaces of Life

One of the greatest thinkers of fifteenth-century Europe was Nicolas of Cusa (1401–1464). Nicolas brought ideas from philosophy, mathematics, and ecumenical theology together into a cohesive whole. The breadth of Nicolas's writing and research remains influential to this day. One of his better-known writings is *De Vision Dei* (*The Vision of God*). In it, he writes that for the human to see the face of God, we have to see past the "face" of the world around us. He says, "As regards to whoever sets out to see Your Face: as long as they conceive of something, they are far removed from Your Face."[8] In other words, in order for us to see the invisible God, we have to see invisibly. It's having eyes to see and ears to hear between the spaces of life on earth. It's a continual awareness of Christ in us and Christ through us in every nanosecond of our lives. When we have this perspective of life, our priorities reflect it. We don't desire all the world has to offer because we know it's fleeting.

A couple of years ago, my wife and I decided it was time to simplify our lives, particularly during the Advent and Christmas seasons. Instead of unloading nine or ten giant tubs of Christmas decorations to place around the house, we would instead put up a tree with just a few sentimental ornaments. Like others, we had fulfilled cultural holiday obligations for decorating our homes inside and out and by purchasing dozens of gifts when we should have been preparing ourselves for the arrival of the baby. The result of our shift was an Advent and Christmas focused not on decorating for the holiday season, but on preparing ourselves for the birth of the Savior of the world.

One December day, I had to go into a giant store to make a purchase. From the moment I entered the crowded store, I became overwhelmed by the seemingly thousands of decorations, musical toys, and bustling multitudes of miserable-looking people filling their shopping carts with the latest plastic action figures and video games. Rather than feeling in the festive holiday mood, I felt dazed and burdened for all these people who allowed cultural expectations to guide their energies and finances. I made my purchase and left the store as dozens of people were crowding in. I wanted to warn them that they were heading into a trap and to guard their hearts. As I sat in my cold car in that parking lot, I began to think of all the ways we spend our energies on things that don't have eternal significance, and then wonder why our lives are filled with stress and exhaustion.

Not Situation, but Perspective

Before we're ready to invite the Holy Spirit to overhaul the complexities of daily life, we must make sure that we're ready. To paraphrase Chautard,

8. Nicolas, *The Vision of God*, 6.21.

fruitful, holy, external activities must first come from a transformed, devoted inner life.[9] The grace of God extends to the depths of God's knowledge of us. Our spirit may be willing, but our flesh may be weak (Mark 14:38). Not everyone is ready for life in the fourth degree of prayer. A new snow skier must begin on the bunny slope before she can advance to the green, blue, or even black slopes. We need to be able to digest spiritual milk before we're ready for spiritual meat (1 Corinthians 3:2). How, then, might we begin to live with this perspective?

The spiritual insight of John Wesley and the early Methodists came from his deep understanding of the human condition. Wesley himself had been ordained a priest in the Church of England, yet he wrote later in life that at his ordination he didn't have faith in Christ. While at Oxford, Wesley and other students met for what was called the "Holy Club." It consisted of marking every time one sinned through the day and by being vulnerable to each other to confess these sins. The legalism inherent in this group was palpable.

After his conversion experience in 1738, Wesley renovated the precepts of the Holy Club to incorporate more than behavior modification. Depending on the degree of one's relationship with Christ, Wesley's Methodists met in either a class, which focused on outward behavior, or a band, which dealt with the inner workings of the human soul. Wesley understood that having others in our lives to be the voice of God to us is essential for having an eternal perspective of human existence. For those of us not in a class or band meeting today, Wesley offers a simple, yet weighty exhortation: "Do nothing on which you cannot pray for a blessing."[10] The light of Christ shines through us into a dark world when followers of Christ observe this straightforward maxim.

Not Results, but Motivation

Nineteenth-century abolitionist and African missionary Cardinal Charles Lavigerie is reputed to have said, "There is no halfway between holiness and absolute perversion."[11] If this is true, then the thin line that exists between the two is motivation. When our motivations for living a holy life are pure, the outcome is love. Conversely, when our motivation for holy living is

9. Chautard, *The Soul of the Apostolate*, 74.

10. Wesley, Sermon CV, 194.

11. As quoted in Chautard, *The Soul of the Apostolate*, 75.

so others might see our holiness, the outcome is typically prideful, pious snobbery. A person living in the fourth degree of prayer cares not how they appear to others. In fact, several of the church fathers write that they desire to be seen as the most unworthy of sinners rather than the holiest person in the community. I've often told my students that when I was a studying at Asbury Seminary, it was common for students to implicitly attempt to out-holy each other. In our competitive world, it's common for us to compare our lives with others, even in terms of discipleship. If we're honest with ourselves, we'll see that we all struggle with this on a certain level. Even Jesus' own disciples wanted to know who was the greatest among them (Luke 22:24). The Savior's response was probably not what they desired to hear.

Likewise, we need to be mindful of how we encourage and exhort others in the faith without appearing to be condemning. Even if we are living without regard for our reputation or status in the community, others are not yet to that point. We may find ourselves compelled by the Spirit to have a hard conversation with someone who is making self-destructive decisions. We must be careful in our interactions with them, speaking truth in love (Ephesians 4:15) and flavoring our dialogue with love and humility. Our motivation is a key point here. Wesley was keenly aware of the tenderness of these conversations, but he was also resolute in our responsibility to have them: "Love indeed requires us to warn [someone], not only of sin . . . but likewise of any error which . . . would naturally lead to sin . . . If we love our neighbor as ourselves, this will be our constant endeavor; to warn him [or her] of every evil way, and of every mistake which tends to evil."[12] If we truly love someone, the state of their soul is our responsibility. If we're living in the fourth degree of prayer, the Holy Spirit will keep our approach pure and selfless.

If purity and selflessness are not the motivating elements in our exhortational conversations, we reveal to ourselves that we have not given our heart, soul, or mind to Christ. We live out of impure motivations when the outcomes of any activity or conversation ends up back with us. A life in the fourth degree of prayer is always focused away from ourselves and into the lives of others. We give thanks to God when God blesses us with insights and consolations, but when we are enraptured in the intimate arms of God, personal gain has no value to us.

---

12. Wesley, Sermon LXV, 297.

A Living Embrace of Christ

One of my favorite paintings is "Christ Embracing St. Bernard," by the Spaniard Francesco Ribalta (1565–1628). Painted near the end of his life, the striking image solicits the viewer to ponder the deep love between Bernard and Jesus, who has come down from the cross to embrace the Cistercian abbot. One's eye is immediately drawn to Bernard's face as his head rests gently on Jesus' arm. His expression is one of absolute contentment and bliss. His right hand hangs limply from Jesus' other arm. Bernard has no concern with any stress of life. All that matters is that he is resting contently in Jesus' arms. What amazes me about this painting is what appears after we have meditated upon the image for a few minutes. In the background, hidden in the shadows, faces seem to appear. The expression on these faces are quite different from Bernard's expression. They are people who look at this embrace in wonder and contemplation. The love between Bernard and the crucified Jesus has affected them so profoundly that they are examining their own love for Christ. We don't realize how brightly Bernard is shining until we look at the faces of those in the background. One might even observe that the faces are looking back at us, beckoning us to self-examination. All the while, Bernard remains fixed on Jesus, paying no heed to the look of marvel on the faces of those observing him.

In the fourth degree of prayer, the focus of our lives is like that of Bernard in Jesus' arms. We aren't removed from the world or hiding our light from the world (Matthew 5:15). Rather, we don't allow the distractions of the world interfere with our embrace of Christ. Bernard's life was one of action and of contemplation. He knew how to engage the ills of society without society negatively affecting his deeply cherished love of Jesus. As a Cistercian monk, Bernard had already forsaken the world. His initial call from God to remain cloistered from society became muddled as he was beckoned by bishops, popes, and kings to engage political and ecclesiastical scandals. While these engagements negatively affected his already frail body, they only deepened his love for Christ and his unique ministerial calling.

Those of us without a monastic call still have a general call from Christ to take up our cross and die to ourselves (Luke 14:27). We're called to avoid the enticements of the world (1 John 2:16). We're called to keep our eyes on Jesus, the author and perfecter of our faith (Hebrews 12:2). These marks of a disciple of Jesus come from an eternal view of our lives. We are eternal beings, created by an eternal God, redeemed by an eternal Savior, and filled with an eternal Spirit. Regardless of how we want to craft ourselves otherwise, this is who we are. In the words of C. S. Lewis, "Nature is mortal; we shall out-live her. When all the suns and nebulae have passed away, each one of you will still be alive."[13] With this perspective, life in the fourth degree of prayer doesn't seem so unreachable after all. It begins in the will, is processed with holy motivation, and is realized by the Holy Spirit as an intimate relationship with God.

Not Planning, but Living

Living in the fourth degree of prayer offers a life of peace, regardless of our present circumstances. I tend to overplan and overthink situations, so finding contentment has been an issue for me throughout the years. "If I plan this event to the nth degree, I can be prepared for all possible circumstances." "I needed to tweak the words in that email for thirty minutes so it would say exactly what I wanted it to convey." This desire for perfection demonstrates restlessness in us. This restlessness comes from an implicit desire to control. Control is the opposite of how we should view our lives. Merton writes in *Thoughts in Solitude* that we need "to stop thinking about how to live and begin to live."[14] We focus so intently on perfecting our walk with Christ that we fail to walk with Christ. It's like pastors who are so concerned about how to please everyone in their congregations that they forget to be a pastor.

Many years ago I knew a man who was a baseball pitcher at the minor league level. He said he tried so hard to throw a perfect pitch that he realized one day that he had forgotten how to throw the ball. This can happen to us as our relationship with Christ deepens into the third and fourth degrees of prayer. We overthink what a disciple of Jesus looks like so we try diligently not to fail God. The Son of God became incarnate, savingly died on the cross for us, rose from the dead so we can have eternal life, and ascended into heaven so we might follow him there. Yet we worry and stress about praying out loud in a group because we might say the wrong thing.

If we wish to be honest with ourselves, our spiritual restlessness comes from insecurity, when we should have assurance of our relationship with Christ. Rabbi Meir S. Dvim once said, "When you don't know God, there are no answers. When you do know God, there are no longer any

13. Lewis, *The Weight of Glory and Other Addresses*, 43–44.
14. Merton, *Thoughts in Solitude*, 84.

questions."[15] If we are still searching anxiously for life's answers, we prove to ourselves that we haven't yet surrendered all of who we are to Christ: our souls, our hearts, our minds, our personalities, our dreams, our families, everything. Perhaps this is why Bernard of Clairvaux writes that curiosity is the first step on the ladder of pride.[16] When we do forfeit all of these to the divine providence of God, we find the peace that surpasses all human understanding that Paul references in Philippians 4:7.

When we die to Christ and he raises us anew, our striving to live the perfect life dissipates and we live completely and freely in the Holy Spirit. It's then that we're able to produce spiritual fruit to edify others. Chautard reminds us that "only a really interior person of works will have enough life to produce other centers of fruitful life."[17] It's the action of the Holy Spirit in the deepest recesses of our lives that produces the *hortus solo*, or garden soil, for the fruit of the Spirit to grow.

Becoming a Singing Soul

If you've ever sung a hymn or other worship song and then later read the words out loud without the music, you quickly realize that without the music, a bit of emotive meaning is lost. St. Augustine writes that "he who sings praise is not only singing, but also loving Him to whom he is singing."[18] I'd like to think that life in the fourth degree of prayer is a hymn of praise to God. Psalm 100 tells us to "make a joyful noise unto the Lord . . . Serve the Lord with gladness: come before his presence with singing." If our lives were a song to God, my hunch is that many of us would be so concerned about singing well that we wouldn't be able to sing with abandon. The grace for us is that Psalm 100 exhorts us to sing joyfully rather than perfectly. The Christian worship band Delirious has phrased it this way:

> We're standing still
> In a moment of eternity
> Where worlds collide
> And I feel the breath of heaven over me
> My soul sings, my soul sings.[19]

15. Quoted by Jill Carter, in personal communication with the author.
16. Bernard, *The Steps of Humility and Pride*.
17. Chautard, *The Soul of the Apostolate*, 151.
18. Augustine, *Exposition on the Psalms*, 334.
19. Garrard et al., "My Soul Sings."

The soul of someone living in the fourth degree of prayer is one that sings incarnationally between the worlds of heaven and earth. It's an existence in two worlds at once. When we live in the fourth degree of prayer, our soul sings praises to God without us even having to make an effort. Rather than striving to maintain our relationship with God, we're able to live in the freedom of having surrendered ourselves to the very one who created us, who saved us, and who empowers us for countercultural faithfulness.

A soul sings when it discovers its true identity in Christ and is thus freed to live a life of joy in holy love, regardless of our present circumstances. A soul sings in our humanity, which God exalts above all other creation because the Son of God himself became a human.[20] A soul sings with justice for it is righteous before God. A soul sings with temperance, for it desires God rather than the world. A soul sings with prudence, for it is filled with wisdom from the Holy Spirit. A soul sings with fortitude, for it requires steadfastness to walk one direction when the world is heading another. A soul that sings encompasses faith, hope, and love to such depths that it remains solidly fixed on Jesus, even when the world seems to be crashing down around us. All of this, and more, is the fourth degree of prayer.

20. For a beautiful explication of this theme, see Bernard, *Sermons for Advent.*

Bibliography

Alter, Adam. *Irresistible: The Rise of Addictive Technology and the Business of Keeping Us Hooked*. New York: Penguin, 2017.

Ambrose of Milan. *De Isaac vel anima (On Isaac and the Soul)*. Corpus Scriptorum Ecclesiasticorum Latinorum. 13 vols. Vienna, 1897.

———. *Of the Sacraments*. In *Theological and Dogmatic Works: The Mysteries, The Holy Spirit, The Incarnation, The Sacraments*. Translated by Roy J. Deferarri. Washington, DC: Catholic University of America Press, 1963.

———. *On the Holy Spirit*. In *Theological and Dogmatic Works: The Mysteries, The Holy Spirit, The Incarnation, The Sacraments*. Translated by Roy J. Deferarri. Washington, DC: Catholic University of America Press, 1963.

Aquinas, Thomas. *Summa Theologica: Complete English Edition in Five Volumes*. Translated by Fathers of the English Dominican Province. New York: Benziger Bros., 1948.

Arendt, Hannah. *The Human Condition*. Chicago: University of Chicago Press, 1958.

Athanasius of Alexandria. *On the Incarnation*. Translated by John Behr. Yonkers, NY: St. Vladimir's Seminary Press, 2011.

Augustine of Hippo. *Exposition on the Psalms*. In *Nicene and Post-Nicene Fathers, First Series*, vol. 8, edited by Philip Schaff. Peabody, MA: Hendrickson, 2004.

———. *On the Trinity*. Edited by Gareth B. Matthews. Cambridge: Cambridge University Press, 2002.

———. *Soliloquies*. Edited by Michael P. Foley. New Haven, CT: Yale University Press, 2020.

Ayers, Lewis. *Augustine and the Trinity*. Cambridge: Cambridge University Press, 2010.

Benedict of Nursia. *Rule*. Edited by Timothy Fry. Collegeville, MN: Liturgical, 1981.

Bernard of Clairvaux. *Cistercians and Cluniacs: St. Bernard's Apology to Abbot William*. Translated by Michael Casey. Kalamazoo, MI: Cistercian, 1970.

———. *Five Books on Consideration: Advice to a Pope*. Translated by John D. Anderson and Elizabeth T. Kennan. Kalamazoo, MI: Cistercian, 1976.

———. *The Letters of St. Bernard of Clairvaux*. Translated by Bruno Scott James. Spencer, MA: Cistercian, 1998.

———. *Monastic Sermons*. Translated by Daniel Griggs. Collegeville, MN: Liturgical, 2016.

———. *On Loving God*. Translated by Emero Stiegman. Kalamazoo, MI: Cistercian, 1995.

———. *The Parables & The Sentences*. Translated by Michael Casey. Kalamazoo, MI: Cistercian, 2000.

———. *Sermons on the Song of Songs*. Translated by Kilian Walsh. Collegeville, MN: Cistercian, 1971.

_____. *Sermons for Advent and the Christmas Season*. Translated by Irene Edmonds et al. Kalamazoo, MI: Cistercian, 2007.

_____. *The Steps of Humility and Pride*. Kalamazoo, MI: Cistercian, 1973.

Calvin, John. *Institutes*. Translated by Boniface Ramsey. New York: Newman, 2000.

Casey, Michael. *Grace on the Journey to God*. Brewster, MA: Paraclete, 2018.

Cassaude, Jean Pierre de. *Abandonment to Divine Providence*. Translated by E. J. Strickland. San Francisco: Ignatius, 2011.

Chautard, Jean-Baptiste. *The Soul of the Apostolate*. Translated by a Monk of Our Lady of Gethsemani. Trappist, KY: Ave Maria, 1946.

_____. *The Spirit of Simplicity*. Translated by a Cistercian Monk of Our Lady of Gethsemani. Cincinnati: Joseph Berning, 1948.

Chrysostom, John. *Homilies on the Gospel of St. John*. Edited by Philip Schaff. Buffalo, NY: Christian Literature Co., 1886.

Ciszek, Walter, and Daniel L. Flaherty. *He Leadeth Me: An Extraordinary Testament of Faith*. New York: Image, 2014.

Dorotheos of Gaza. *Discourses and Sayings*. Translated by Eric P. Wheeler. Collegeville, MN: Cistercian, 1977.

Dougherty, Rose Marie. *Group Spiritual Direction: Community for Discernment*. Mahwah, NJ: Paulist, 1995.

Elhai, Jon D., et al. "The Relationship Between Anxiety Symptom Severity and Problematic Smartphone Use: A Review of the Literature and Conceptual Frameworks." *Journal of Anxiety Disorders* 62 (November 30, 2018) 45–52.

Feldman, Christina. *The Buddhist Path to Simplicity*. London: Harper/Thorsons, 2001.

Foster, Richard. *Prayer: Finding the Heart's True Home*. New York: HarperOne, 1992.

Gallup, Inc. "U.S. Church Membership Falls Below Majority for First Time." March 29, 2021. https://news.gallup.com/poll/341963/church-membership-falls-below-majority-first-time.aspx.

Garrard, Stuart, et al. "My Soul Sings." Kingdom of Comfort. Copyright ©2008. Curious? Music UK (PR5) adm. in the US and Canada at CapitolCMGPublishing.com. All rights reserved. Used by permission.

General Chapter of the Cistercian Order. *The Spirit of Simplicity: Characteristic of the Cistercian Order*. Trappist, KY: Ave Maria, 1948.

Gregory I. *Morals on the Book of Job*. Translated by James Bliss. Cambridge, MA: Harvard University Press, 1950.

Gregory of Nyssa. "On the Creation of Man." In *Nicene and Post-Nicene Fathers, Vol. 5*. Edited by Philip Schaff and Henry Wace. Peabody, MA: Hendrickson, 2004.

Halík, Tomáš. *Patience with God: The Story of Zacchaeus Continuing in Us*. New York: Doubleday, 2009.

Hildegard of Bingen. *Scivias*. Translated by Mark Atherton. London: Penguin, 2001.

Hippolytus of Rome. *On the Apostolic Tradition*. Translated by Alistair C. Stewart. Yonkers, NY: St. Vladimir's Seminary Press, 2015.

Irenaeus. *Against Heresies*. In *Ante-Nicene Fathers*, vol. I. Edited by Alexander Roberts and James Donaldson. Grand Rapids: Eerdmans, 2004.

Jobs, Steve. "Apple Press Event Keynote Address." Cupertino, CA, January 27, 2010.

John of the Cross. *The Dark Night (of the Soul)*. Translated by E. Allison Peers. Westminster, MD: Newman, 1953.

Julian of Norwich. *Revelations of Divine Love*. Translated by Elizabeth Spearing. London: Penguin, 1999.

Kreider, Alan. *The Patient Ferment of the Early Church.* Grand Rapids: Baker Academic, 2016.

Laird, Martin. *Into the Silent Land: A Guide to the Christian Practice of Contemplation.* Oxford: Oxford University Press, 2006.

Lewis, C. S. *The Weight of Glory and Other Addresses.* New York: HarperCollins, 1976.

Luther, Martin. *Lectures on Romans.* Luther's Works Volume 25. Edited by Hilton C. Oswald. St. Louis, MO: Concordia, 1972.

McColman, Carl. *Befriending Silence.* Notre Dame, IN: Ave Maria, 2015.

Merton, Thomas. "On Prayer." Darjeeling, Thailand: Unpublished ms., 1968.

_____. *Thoughts in Solitude.* New York: Noonday, 1958.

_____. *Zen and the Birds of Appetite.* New York: New Directions, 1968.

Meyer, Christelle, et. al. "Seasonality in Human Cognitive Brain Responses." *Proceedings of the National Academy of Sciences of the United States of America* 113:11 (2016) 3066–71.

Milne, A. A. *When We Were Very Young.* London: Methuen & Co., 1924.

Mulholland, Robert. *Shaped by the Word: The Power of Scripture in Spiritual Formation.* Nashville: Upper Room, 2001.

Nédoncelle, Maurice. *God's Encounter with Man: A Contemporary Approach to Prayer.* New York: Sheed and Ward, 1964.

Nicolas of Cusa. *The Vision of God.* Translated by H. Lawrence Bond. Mahwah, NJ: Paulist, 1997.

Okholm, Dennis. *Monk Habits for Everyday People.* Grand Rapids: Brazos, 2007.

Palmer, Phoebe. *The Promise of the Father: Or, A Neglected Specialty of the Last Days, Addressed to the Clergy and Laity of All Christian Communities.* Eugene, OR: Wipf and Stock, 2015.

Pew Research Center. "In U.S., Decline of Christianity Continues at Rapid Pace: An update on America's changing religious landscape." October 17, 2019. https://www.pewforum.org/2019/10/17/in-u-s-decline-of-christianity-continues-at-rapid-pace/.

Proceedings of the National Academy of Sciences of the United States of America 113:11 (March 15, 2016) 3066–71.

Steere, Douglas V. *Dimensions of Prayer.* New York: Harper & Row, 1963.

Sterne, Alastair. *Rhythms for Life: Spiritual Practices for Who God Made You to Be.* Downers Grove, IL: InterVarsity, 2020.

Teresa of Avila. *Interior Castle.* Translated by E. Allison Peers. New York: Image, 1989.

Theodoret of Cyrus. *Commentary on the Song of Songs.* Translated by Robert C. Hill. Brisbane: Australian Catholic University, 2001.

Thomas à Kempis. *The Imitation of Christ.* Translated by Joseph N. Tylenda. New York: Vintage, 1998.

Underhill, Evelyn. *Practical Mysticism.* Columbus, OH: Ariel, 1986.

Ward, Benedicta, ed. *The Sayings of the Desert Fathers: The Alphabetical Collection.* Kalamazoo, MI: Cistercian, 1984.

Wesley, John. *Explanatory Notes Upon the New Testament.* New York: Lane and Tippett, 1845.

_____. Letter DCCIX, "To Miss Bishop." In *Wesley's Works,* vol. XIII. Peabody, MA: Hendrickson, 1991.

_____. *A Plain Account of Christian Perfection.* In *Wesley's Works,* vol. XI. Peabody, MA: Hendrickson, 1991.

_____. Sermon XVI. In *Wesley's Works,* vol. V. Peabody, MA: Hendrickson, 1991.

_____. Sermon XXVI. In *Wesley's Works,* vol. V. Peabody, MA: Hendrickson, 1991.

_____. Sermon XXX. In *Wesley's Works,* vol. V. Peabody, MA: Hendrickson, 1991.

_____. Sermon LXV. In *Wesley's Works,* vol. II. Peabody, MA: Hendrickson, 1991.

_____. Sermon CV. In *Wesley's Works,* vol. III. Peabody, MA: Hendrickson, 1991.

_____. Sermon CXL. In *Wesley's Works,* vol. III. Peabody, MA: Hendrickson, 1991.

William of St. Thierry. *The Golden Epistle.* Translated by Theodore Berkeley. Kalamazoo, MI: Cistercian, 1971.

Wimberly, C. F. *A Biographical Sketch of Henry Clay Morrison D.D.: Editor of "The Pentecostal Herald," the Man and His Ministry*. Wilmore, KY: First Fruits, 2012.

CPSIA information can be obtained
at www.ICGtesting.com
Printed in the USA
LVHW031757300122
709788LV00005B/316